CULTURES

TURKEY

Sean Sheehan

MARSHALL CAVENDISH
New York • London • Sydney

Reference edition published 1993 by
Marshall Cavendish Corporation
2415 Jerusalem Avenue
P.O. Box 587
North Bellmore
New York 11710

© Times Editions Pte Ltd 1993

Originated and designed by
Times Books International, an imprint of
Times Editions Pte Ltd

Printed in Singapore

Library of Congress Cataloging-in-Publication Data:
Sheehan, Sean,
    Turkey / Sean Sheehan.
      p. cm.—(Cultures Of The World)
    Includes bibliographical references and index.
    Summary: Describes the geography, history,
government, economy, and culture of Turkey.
    ISBN 1-85435-576-7
    1. Turkey—Juvenile literature [1. Turkey.]
I. Title. II. Series.
DR417.D54 1993
956.1—dc20   92–35930
                          CIP
                           AC

Cultures of the World

Editorial Director	Shirley Hew
Managing Editor	Shova Loh
Editors	Leonard Lau
	Tan Kok Eng
	Michael Spilling
	Sue Sismondo
Picture Editor	Yee May Kaung
Production	Edmund Lam
Design	Tuck Loong
	Ronn Yeo
	Felicia Wong
	Loo Chuan Ming
Illustrators	Jimmy Kang
	Kelvin Sim
	Philip Lim
MCC Editorial Director	Evelyn M. Fazio

INTRODUCTION

TURKEY lies both in Europe and Asia. It is open to the cultural and economic forces of Western and Eastern Europe. At the same time, it is exposed to the ancient cultures of the Middle East. This geographical uniqueness has meant that fascinating and diverse influences have contributed to the country's historical and cultural development. With the breakup of the Soviet Union, Turkey is now reaching out to the new autonomous states on its eastern borders.

Surrounded by such dissimilar cultures, it is not surprising that Turkey has evolved its own very appealing identity. It is Moslem, very traditional, and Asian in some respects, but also highly industrialized, forward-looking, and metropolitan in other ways.

This book, part of the *Cultures of the World* series, provides an insight into the complex and appealing lifestyle of the Turks—their work, leisure, attitudes, value systems, cuisine, and culture.

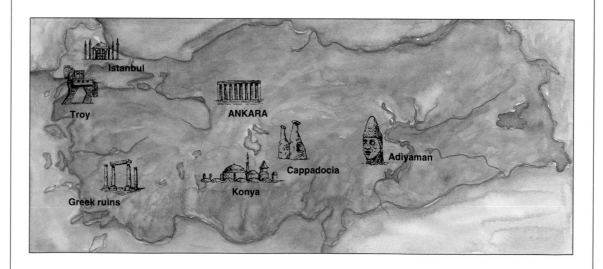

CONTENTS

A large stone carving of King Antiochus near Adiyaman, southern Turkey.

CONTENTS

A Turkish woman in Pamukkale, western Turkey.

GEOGRAPHY

TURKEY LIES PARTLY in Europe and partly in Asia. The European region is known as Thrace, while the Asian region is Anatolia. Thrace is 9,000 square miles in area. This is small compared with Anatolia's 300,000 square miles.

Turkey is bounded on the west by Greece, Bulgaria, and the Aegean Sea; on the east by Iran and the former Soviet Union; and on the south by Iraq, Syria, and the Mediterranean Sea. It is bordered by the Black Sea on the north. European Turkey is separated from Asian Turkey by the Bosporus, the Sea of Marmara, and the Dardanelles Strait.

THE NATURAL ENVIRONMENT

The central mass of Turkey, known as the Central Anatolian Plateau, is surrounded by the Pontic Mountains to the north and the Taurus Mountains to the south. There are mountain ridges to the west and the east as well. Cut off from rain-bearing winds by mountain ranges, the central plateau is semi-arid. Less than 10% of Turkey consists of level or gently sloping lands. The climate varies greatly, due to the differing geographies. The Black Sea region to the north has a temperate climate with warm summers and mild winters. The western Aegean coastline and the southern Mediterranean shores have hot summers, and do not have the freezing winters of the interior. Not surprisingly, most tourists are attracted to the coastal regions. There, the average annual temperature is around 68°F. Summer temperatures can reach 84°F.

Above: **A road leads through the Pontic Mountains to the Black Sea. Dense pine forests cover the slopes of the mountains.**

Opposite: **The thermal spring waters of Pamukkale are renowned for their therapeutic powers. Laden with salt, these waters have calcified to form basins and dazzling white petrified cascades.**

Boats moored along the Black Sea coast. Where natural shelters are not available, artificial shelters are constructed to provide safe anchorage to boats.

THE BLACK SEA COAST

The Black Sea coast extends along the northern margins of the country, from Uskudar in the west to the former Soviet frontier in the east. Geographically, the whole area is influenced by the mountain range that lies just behind the thin coastal strip of land. Hot air moving over the coast rises to cross the mountains. But as it does, the higher altitude causes it to cool and fall as rain. Consequently, the Black Sea coast is the wettest part of Turkey. Only July and August are hot in this region.

Three of Europe's longest rivers flow into the Black Sea: the Don, the Dnieper, and the Danube. Powerful currents carry the waters through the Bosporus—the only outlet for the Black Sea. The Bosporus is a short strait, 19 miles long, that connects the Black Sea with the Sea of Marmara.

Where the rivers flow into the Black Sea, the level of salt in the water is very low. This makes the sea water here almost drinkable. However, in the southern part of the sea there is a vast underwater pool of salty, stagnant water that makes it difficult for marine life to survive.

The Pontic Mountains in this region follow the contour of the southern shore of the Black Sea. The slopes of the mountains that descend to the coast are covered in thick woods. The timber harvested from these woods

is used for building houses and boats. Many of the villages in this region have a tradition of boatbuilding. Boats provide the means for fishing. During the winter, large quantities of Black Sea anchovies are caught and sold.
— The geography of the coast is such that bays are rare, and natural harbors do not exist. People who make their living from the sea have had to develop the skill of handling small boats in rough weather without the benefit of safe harbors.

Hemmed in by the Pontic Mountains on one side and the Black Sea on the other, the city of Trabzon spreads along a narrow strip of flat land.

The mountains have also served to make this part of Turkey isolated and inaccessible. As a result, various ethnic groups have managed to survive and, until very recently, contact with the rest of Turkey has been minimal. The absence of any industry has made the region very dependent on agriculture. Crop failure often spells disaster.

In the past, mineral deposits around the region of Sinop on the coast attracted adventurers and entrepreneurs. The legendary Jason and the Argonauts explored this part of Turkey in their search for gold and other valuable minerals. Today, it is said that villagers still place sheepskins in the streams hoping to collect traces of gold dust.

The most interesting city along the Black Sea coast is the ancient settlement of Trabzon. Known as Trebizond in the past, it was the seat of an empire fabled for its wealth. Today, Trabzon has a strong tourist industry.

Abounding in beautiful beaches and olive groves, the Aegean coast has one of the loveliest landscapes in Turkey.

THE AEGEAN REGION

The Aegean region, extending from the Dardanelles in the north to Rhodes in the south, is one of the most advanced regions of Turkey. The Aegean coast has attracted visitors for centuries. Indeed, many modern tourists come to this part of Turkey to visit the antiquities that belonged to the visitors of centuries past: the ancient Greeks and the Romans. They also come to enjoy the summer sun, splendid beaches, and beautiful holiday villages.

Long ago, geography attracted outsiders to this part of Turkey. The plains inland from the Aegean coast form some of the richest land in the country. Many of Turkey's export crops, such as olives, tobacco, grapes, and figs, flourish in the hospitable climate and accommodating soil.

The main cities in the Aegean region are Izmir, Manisa, and Aydin.

THE MEDITERRANEAN REGION

Turkey's Mediterranean region extends from Rhodes to the Syrian frontier. This region is dominated by mountains. The Taurus Mountains rise to a height of over 10,000 feet. The fine scenery and beautiful beaches have given this area the name "the Turquoise Coast."

The mountains here have also given rise to the Chimera, known since the days of the ancient Greeks. The Chimera is a natural flame produced by the burning of gases that escape from the face of the rocks. Oil technologists have studied it, hoping that it would lead to large deposits of oil, but only traces of methane were detected. The Chimera

was also a name given to a fire-breathing monster that was believed to inhabit the mountains.

Along the extreme western Mediterranean coast, the Taurus Mountains make the area largely inaccessible to those without a boat or yacht. However, along the eastern Mediterranean coast, the Taurus Mountains do not reach as far as the sea. A fertile plain has helped develop the region around the port of Antalya. The sunny climate and unspoiled beaches have attracted visitors in the thousands.

To the east of Antalya, mountains again predominate. This area was renowned in the past for its pirates and dangerous shores. Farther along, on the other side of the mountains, is the separate plain of Cilicia. This is now a prosperous part of Turkey, largely due to its production of cotton for export. It is close to Syria, and there are many social and cultural links. A significant number of Arabs live in this part of Turkey.

Situated on top of cliffs overlooking a crescent-shaped bay, Antalya is the chief tourist resort on the Turkish Riviera.

11

Rugged, hilly terrain is a common feature of the semi-arid Central Anatolian Plateau.

ANATOLIA

Anatolia includes the Central Anatolian Plateau and the eastern and southeastern parts of Turkey that have no coastline.

Central Anatolia is a forbidding mixture of desert and grasslands, hot in the summer and freezing during the winter. Hardy goats and sheep graze on the poor soil. Water is often scarce during the summer months, except in areas where irrigation has been introduced. Nearly all the arable land is used to grow grain.

In the south, a distinctive feature of the landscape is the number of lakes lying between mountains. A high salt content and the ever-present

Lake Van as seen from Aktamar, one of the many islands found on the lake. Lake Van has a high saline content and is practically devoid of animal life.

danger of flooding have discouraged communities from settling near these lakes. Nevertheless, people have lived in central Anatolia for millennia.

Southeastern Anatolia is a barren plateau drained by the Tigris and the Euphrates rivers. The land is poor, and this is the least economically advanced region of Turkey. Hopes are pinned on the early completion of a dam on the Euphrates that would transform the area into land fit for agriculture. At the moment, the Euphrates Basin, with its rich alluvial deposits, provides the only decent land for cultivation.

The bare pristine stones of southeastern Anatolia provided the material for what is probably the most famous image of classical Turkey: the detached heads and truncated figures found in the tomb and temple complex at Nemrut Dagi.

Eastern Anatolia is the least populated region of Turkey. It has fewer than 13 people per square mile. This is in stark contrast to the population density of 500 people per square mile along the Black Sea coast. The heart of this region is Lake Van, a huge expanse of water covering 1,443 square miles. Mountains sit all around the lake that fills what was once a lowland basin. When a nearby volcano erupted, the lava blocked off the basin area and formed the present-day lake.

CAPPADOCIA

The most fascinating region of Anatolia is Cappadocia. The land of Cappadocia is composed of soft volcanic rock that came from the eruptions of volcanoes 30 million years ago. The soft rock has succumbed to the force of erosion, and the resulting weird formations are known as fairy chimneys.

Even more spectacular are the remains of underground cities that have been carved out of the rock. One river valley, the Ihlara Valley, even has churches cut into its sides.

UNDERGROUND CITIES

The underground cities of Cappadocia are believed to be more than 2,000 years old. This is quite amazing when one considers that some of them are capable of holding up to 25,000 people. They were probably constructed first for defensive purposes, but later communities adapted them as permanent homes, schools, and churches.

Only some parts of the subterranean cities are open to the public, but it is enough to create astonishment and respect for those who built and lived in them. The original ventilation system is still adequate to allow groups of tourists to explore the remains 164 feet below the ground. It is possible to recognize what were once stables and wine cellars. One room contains two large stone-cut tables that may have functioned as a school room or communal dining area. A complex series of channels connects the many floor levels, with the deeper levels containing the dungeons. Extraordinary escape routes have been traced, one leading a distance of nearly six miles underground.

THE MOUNTAIN OF NOAH

Although Turkey is basically made up of mountains, the most famous mountain in the country is not noted for its great height but rather for what landed on its summit.

Mount Ararat, rising to 16,786 feet, is traditionally associated with the mountain on which Noah's Ark came to rest after the Flood. It is situated close to the border with Iran (formerly Persia), and the Iranian name for the mountain is "Koh-i-Nur," the Mountain of Noah.

Ararat is a volcanic mountain with two peaks, Great Ararat and Little Ararat, that are separated by a distance of some seven miles. Snow is found on the higher slopes. Most of the lower slopes contain pasture.

This region of Turkey was once peopled by Armenians. According to Armenian monks, the mountain was a sacred place that was not to be climbed.

It was not until the early 19th century that anyone was allowed to reach the summit. A German explorer became the first person to be in a position to see whether any remains of Noah's Ark could be found. Neither he nor any subsequent climbers have found any positive evidence to support the biblical account.

Opposite top: **The fairy chimneys of Cappadocia. Dwellings are carved out of these rocks.**

Above: **Mount Ararat forms a scenic backdrop to a cluster of villages.**

FLORA AND FAUNA

Large areas of western and southern Turkey are covered by a Mediterranean-type vegetation, consisting of thick underbrush in the lowlands and deciduous and coniferous forests at higher altitudes. Along the northern margins is the densely wooded region of the country, while on the eastern Black Sea coast is subtropical forest. The country's varied climate has produced a diverse flora. The Mediterranean climate allows characteristic European plants, such as crocuses, to flourish. In central Anatolia, on the other hand, the dry and arid terrain produces a distinctive flora. A high evaporation rate brings salt to the surface of the soil, and plants that normally grow by the seashore, such as the orache, flourish here.

The wooded areas shelter a large number of animals. Turkey boasts a richer fauna than any other country in Europe. There are deer, foxes, wolves, boars, beavers, and hyenas. Even bears still roam secluded parts of the country. Game birds such as partridge, quail, and bustard are common.

Rich, verdant vegetation such as this is found along the northern margins of Turkey.

ISTANBUL

Istanbul is a surprise to many people, especially to visitors from North America or Western Europe. It is situated in Europe and yet has a characteristically Asian feel to it. Many people assume it is still the capital of Turkey and, culturally at least, it has remained so. It also has a larger

population than the capital, Ankara.

Istanbul's skyline is crowded with domes, mosques, and <u>minarets.</u> Two of its most famous buildings highlight its dramatic identity. Aya Sofya, or the Church of the Divine Wisdom, built in the 6th century, represents the Byzantine Christian era, while the Sultan Ahmed Cami, the Blue Mosque, bears testimony to an age when Istanbul was also the capital of an Islamic empire.

Istanbul remains a city of contrasts. It is amazingly busy, with roads, bridges, trains, boats, and planes bringing in travelers from other parts of Turkey and the world. The population is about 10 million, almost 18% of the country's total. Recent estimates indicate that nine out of 10 inhabitants are first-generation city dwellers. Because the population is growing at an alarming rate, Istanbul is badly overcrowded. Traffic congestion is every bit as terrible as in New York City or London.

Despite the overcrowding and inadequate infrastructure, Istanbul has retained its distinctly ancient charm and identity. People still find time to stroll about, or talk for hours in the city's countless coffeehouses.

Istanbul's skyline and ferries. Istanbul is the only city in the world to be built on two continents. It stands on the shores of the Bosporus, where the waters of the Black Sea mingle with those of the Sea of Marmara and the Golden Horn.

ANKARA

Ankara, the capital of Turkey since 1923, offers a dramatic contrast to Istanbul. It has a very modern appearance that is different from the old world charm of Istanbul. In ancient times, Ankara was the site of an important settlement. When Kemal Ataturk, the founder of modern Turkey, chose to establish the nation's capital here, the place was only a small provincial town. However, such has been the pace of development that the city's buildings now reach to the surrounding hills. And the metropolis is still growing. During the harsh Anatolian winter,

Above: **Although Ankara is the seat of government and administration, it is also Turkey's second most important industrial city.**

Opposite: **Traditional Anatolian town houses are built of stone or wood. They are usually two stories high, with the upper story often protruding cantilever fashion into the street.**

a thick smog covers the city, caused by the burning of an enormous amount of coal to keep the inhabitants warm. In the summer months, the heat is intense. A dusty haze often surrounds the city.

The old town still exists but is dwarfed by the shining glass and concrete of the modern capital. The administrative center of the country, Ankara is the headquarters of nearly all the important businesses in the nation. Unemployed people from the surrounding areas come to the capital to search for work, and the city has its share of shanty towns. What started out as temporary dwellings have now become permanent residences. The authorities, realizing they cannot eject thousands of families, have provided a supply of electricity and fresh water. These settlements are now suburbs in their own right, although they look and feel quite different from the middle-class areas. Many of the inhabitants like to keep animals in their small gardens and grow their own vegetables.

HISTORY

TURKEY has a rich and illustrious past, predating the arrival of the Turks in the 11th century. Little is known of the earliest Neolithic inhabitants, although excavations have revealed their wall paintings, including one of a volcano erupting that can claim to be the world's oldest landscape painting. The first people to settle in what is now Turkey, and create what would be called a civilization, were the Hittites. Many more peoples and civilizations were to follow.

THE HITTITES

The Hittite empire, from 1700 to 1200 B.C., was one of the first and most significant settlements in Turkey. The Hittites' center of power was based in central Anatolia at Hattusas, near modern Ankara. The empire came to an end when it succumbed to various tribes from the west in 1200 B.C.

Excavations at Hattusas suggest that the city was enormous. The fortified wall surrounding it was about four miles long. Inside the city, special rooms were set aside for storing written records. The Hittites maintained a professional army and were also artistically inclined. Examples of Hittite rock carvings can still be seen today.

The Hittites were one of the first people to develop a written constitution. Many aspects of their culture show them to be a mature and civilized community. War was only undertaken as a last resort. They had a policy of not torturing and mutilating their prisoners of war. Such attitudes distinguished them from most of their contemporaries in the Middle East.

When the Hittite empire collapsed, a succession of small states followed. Two of these, Phrygia and Lydia, played important roles in the ancient world.

Below: **The Greek amphitheater at Miletus, western Anatolia.**

Opposite top: **A wooden model of the Trojan Horse stands in the ancient city of Troy in northwestern Anatolia. The reality behind the Trojan War was intense commercial rivalry between the Greeks and the north Aegean settlers who built their prosperous city at Troy.**

Opposite bottom: **A mosaic showing Constantine the Great dedicating the church to Jesus Christ.**

THE GREEKS AND THE PERSIANS

Crossing the Aegean Sea, the Greeks came as traders. By 900 B.C., they had settled along the western shores of Anatolia. Greek colonies such as Troy, Ephesus, and Miletus thrived as commercial centers.

By 700 B.C., most of the Greek colonies were subjected to Lydian rule. The most famous king of Lydia was Croesus, who was known as the richest man on earth, an indication of the extent of Lydia's power. Such power, however, attracted the envy of the Persian empire, which conquered Lydia in 546 B.C. The Greek cities of Anatolia came under the control of the Persians for several centuries. It was not until Alexander the Great conquered Anatolia in 334 B.C. that the Greeks were able to reestablish their influence.

THE INFLUENCE OF ROME

After the Greeks came the Romans. As early as 133 B.C., Anatolia had come under Roman rule. Christian apostles, such as Paul and Barnabas, helped Christianize almost all of the country. Major events in the history of the Christian church took place in Anatolia.

In A.D. 330, the Roman emperor Constantine chose the old Greek city of Byzantium as the center for the eastern half of his empire. He renamed

TROY

Known to the world through the ancient Greek epics the *Iliad* and *Odyssey* by Homer, Troy is very much a part of the history of Turkey. An ancient city in northwestern Anatolia, it was the capital of a royal house that once ruled the lands around it.

The remains of Troy (Truva in Turkish) are not as spectacular as the history that lies behind them. Today, the few remains of walls and stones testify to a city that, for a long time, was thought only to exist in the imagination of ancient storytellers.

Legend became reality in 1871 when Heinrich Schliemann, a German merchant turned archeologist, excavated in a part of northwest Turkey. He uncovered nine layers of remains, with each one representing a separate stage in the evolution of the city. The oldest dates back to 3600 B.C., while the last layer was built during the time of the Roman empire. Troy VII, destroyed by fire around 1250 B.C., is probably the city of King Priam described in Homer's *Iliad*.

According to Homer, the war between the Trojans and the Greeks came about after Paris, the son of the king of Troy, abducted Helen, the queen of the Greek city of Sparta. Her irate husband, Menelaus, gathered a host of Greek heroes from other city states to help him recover his wife. Achilles and Odysseus were the most famous of these heroes. Under the leadership of King Agamemnon, they sailed off to Troy to do battle. After 10 years of fighting, the wily Odysseus came up with a plan to trick the Trojans with a wooden horse that allowed the Greeks into the city.

it Constantinople, today's Istanbul. When Rome fell to the Goths in A.D. 476, Constantinople became the sole capital of the Byzantine empire. In the 7th century A.D., Anatolia became part of the Byzantine empire.

The Roman legacy can still be seen in the numerous antiquities that continue to attract thousands of visitors each year. There are more Roman statues, inscriptions, and monuments in Turkey than anywhere else outside of Italy. In fact, the most complete Roman theater is found in Turkey.

A religious school with the characteristic Seljuk portal and pointed arch.

THE COMING OF THE TURKS

An important date in the history of Turkey is 1071, the year the Byzantines were defeated by Turkish tribes at the battle of Malazgirt in eastern Anatolia. These early Turks were probably driven west from their homeland in Central Asia by the Mongols.

The Turks brought Islam into a country that was then mostly Christian. They introduced a spirit of commercial enterprise that resulted in a myriad of caravan routes stretching across modern Turkey and into the Middle East. Along the way, they constructed imposing buildings in which travelers could stop and rest. Some of these 12th-century caravansaries still remain.

In the West, the rise of this new Turkish power, known as the Seljuks after one of their Asian princes, aroused the suspicions of European powers. As a result, Pope Urban II promised spiritual rewards to any warrior willing to fight the Seljuks under a Christian flag. Thus, the First Crusade was launched. In time, another three Crusades were fought. They brought much bloodshed and conflict, although they also allowed valuable cultural contacts to be made between Christianity and Islam.

While the western part of Anatolia, along with the Black Sea and Mediterranean coasts, remained Byzantine territory, the Turkish Seljuk empire developed its own identity in the heart of Anatolia. Seljuk rule came to an end in the 13th century, after it was defeated by invading Mongols. No major power arose to fill the vacuum left by the Seljuks, until the rise of the Ottoman empire, a Turkish power that would last three times longer than the 200-year rule of the Seljuks.

THE OTTOMAN EMPIRE

The Ottoman empire took its name from Osman, the ruler of a small state in Anatolia that expanded into one of the most formidable empires in the world. At the height of its power, Ottoman territory included most of North Africa, Iraq, and large areas of Eastern Europe.

Ottoman influence is seen in the monument on the right, dedicated to Ahmed III who ruled from 1703 to 1730.

The empire's western expansion was halted in 1529, when it failed to capture Vienna, the capital of the Hapsburg empire. Ambitions to expand westward were again checked when a second attempt failed in 1683. This second failure proved more costly as the large domain of Hungary was lost. In 1699, the Ottomans signed their first peace treaty as a defeated power.

Ottoman Turks were Moslems and were viewed as a threat by the Christian rulers of Western Europe, who organized joint campaigns to defeat them. From the 17th century onward, the empire gradually stagnated and declined, finally breaking up after the end of World War I in 1918. It had lasted more than 600 years. Although portrayed by the West as a malign and evil force, the Ottoman empire was no more repressive than the regimes governing Europe.

THE JANISSARIES

In the 14th century, as Ottoman territory began incorporating previously Christian lands, a practice developed of taking a proportion of captured boys and raising them as an elite Moslem corps. Called Janissaries (from *yeniçeri,* the Turkish word for "new troops"), they were initially trained as warriors, but those who showed talent were trained as administrators. For a long time, free-born Moslems were actually ineligible to join this privileged group. It was not until the 17th century, after their numbers seriously declined due to wars against Austria and Persia, that Moslems were allowed to enter this elite group. At the height of their influence, the Janissaries were involved in deposing sultans and creating new ones.

Above: **Suleiman the Magnificent was not only known for his military campaigns, but also for his achievements in the fields of law, literature, art, and architecture.**

Opposite top: **Kemal Ataturk, "Father of the Turks."**

Opposite bottom: **World War I veterans are remembered in the war museum in Canakkale.**

It was Mehmed II, ascending the throne in 1451, who set his sights on the capture of Constantinople. This capital of the old Byzantine empire had managed to remain independent despite being surrounded by Ottoman territory. The city finally succumbed in 1453 after a siege of seven weeks, and was renamed Istanbul.

The Ottoman sultans invariably earned themselves epithets. Mehmed, after the fall of Constantinople, became known as "the Conqueror." His son, Beyazit II, who succeeded to the throne, was called "the Pious." Beyazit II was eventually deposed by his own son, a more aggressive character who earned the title of Selim "the Grim." The sultan who considerably increased the size of the Ottoman empire was Suleiman "the Magnificent."

The Ottoman empire had no constitutional system for choosing a new sultan. For centuries, it was the practice of any new sultan to commit fratricide. All of the sultan's brothers would be immediately killed in an attempt to prevent any rival claims to the throne. Such practices contributed to the West's image of the Ottomans as a devilish and uncivilized empire. On the other hand, the Ottomans never insisted on the forcible conversion to Islam of subject peoples (the Janissaries were a notable exception). Walled cities were controlled by Moslems who usually converted the main church into a mosque, but non-Moslem communities simply withdrew to the suburbs, where they were unmolested.

KEMAL ATATURK

The man who became known as the father of modern Turkey first achieved fame during World War I. When war broke out in 1914, the Ottoman empire joined the Central Powers consisting of Germany, Austria-Hungary, and Bulgaria. A combined force from Britain, Australia, and New Zealand landed on the Gallipoli Peninsula in a determined attempt to force Turkey out of the war. The attempt was unsuccessful. The strength of the Turkish resistance was due to the leadership of a hitherto unknown colonel by the name of Mustafa Kemal, who later adopted the surname Ataturk ("Father of the Turks").

The end of the war left Turkey a defeated nation. When Turkey was invaded by a Greek army, Ataturk led the Turkish resistance once again and managed to repel the invaders. As a national champion, he was able to abolish the sultanate and become the first president of a new Turkish republic in 1923.

The new republic did not include many Armenians, previously a significant element of the population. Of the 1.5 million Armenians, it is estimated that half a million fled the country as refugees while the other 1 million were killed. They were eliminated because the Turks feared the Armenians would help Christian Russia during the war.

Ataturk himself was not personally associated with the massacre of Armenians, and he is still considered a hero in Turkey today. He carried out a fundamental reform of his country. There are few areas of Turkish social and political life unaffected by his reforms.

Ataturk sits in on a classroom session. A brilliant military leader, he was also an enlightened statesman and reformer.

THE REFORMS OF ATATURK

As president of Turkey from 1923 to 1938, Ataturk supervised an extraordinary reform of his country. He was driven by a desire to assert Turkey's identity as a modern state and cast off the negative associations created by the decadent decline of the Ottoman empire. Above all, he was keen to dissociate the state from Islam. This was not just a constitutional matter, for Ataturk believed that a country too closely identified with Islam made its citizens too ready to accept inferior conditions.

Ataturk campaigned against the traditional veil for women and against the turban and fez for men. Laws forbade the wearing of the turban and fez, and required the donning of the European hat.

The Gregorian calendar was introduced to replace the Moslem lunar one. The Islamic law code was replaced by statutes resembling the European legal system. Polygamy was outlawed, and women were given the vote. Both marriage and divorce became matters for the civil courts and not the traditional religious ones.

The European alphabet was introduced in 1928, replacing the traditional Arabic script. A commission was set up to modernize the Turkish language and remove many of its Persian and Arabic words. These reforms paved the way for a massive increase in literacy.

TURKEY TODAY

After World War II and throughout the 1950s, Turkey went through a politically turbulent period. In 1960, a military coup was carried out in the name of liberal democracy. Much to the surprise of the rest of the world, free elections were allowed in 1961.

Unstable governments continued to rule, and a war with Greece over Cyprus was narrowly avoided. The population of Cyprus is one-fifth Turkish, but contrary to the spirit of the island's constitution, the rights of the minority were in danger of being submerged by the Greek majority.

In 1971, there was another military takeover, with a government elected two years later. Trouble over Cyprus flared up again. Turkish troops invaded the northern part of the island to secure concessions on behalf of the Turkish Cypriots. These troops remain in northern Cyprus, while a United Nations peacekeeping force maintains an uneasy cease-fire.

Through the 1970s, political instability continued to plague Turkey. Street fighting between different factions was common, and a third military coup took place in 1980. This bloodless coup was greeted with relief by many civilians. But the new regime turned out to be more repressive than the previous two military governments. In 1983, new elections were held.

Turkey has still not achieved political stability. Political assassinations continue, and Islamic fundamentalism poses a threat. However, during the 1991 Gulf War, the government strongly supported the United Nations sanctions against Iraq. Turkey's international credibility needs to be maintained if it is to gain admission to the European Community and resist the forces that could tear the country apart.

Turkey is a member of the North Atlantic Treaty Organization (NATO) and maintains friendly relations with both the United States and the Commonwealth of Independent States.

GOVERNMENT

TURKEY'S PRESENT DEMOCRATIC system has existed since 1983, when the army permitted a general election after its takeover three years earlier. Today, the possibility of another military coup is remote. Turkey is likely to retain its democratic institutions and become more liberal. During the Cold War, the country was supported by the West as a bulwark against the Soviet Union. This is now history. A new-found confidence is emerging among the country's leaders, and pressure from Islamic fundamentalism is being contained.

GOVERNMENT

Turkey is a republic with an elected president, prime minister, and a Grand National Assembly. Turgut Ozal, the current president, has exerted considerable influence on the country's affairs. His right-wing party, known as ANAP, or the Motherland Party, has been in power since winning the general election in 1983. Until October 1989, Ozal was the prime minister. When he became president, opponents objected on the grounds that, unlike the situation in the United States, the presidency should not be held by someone with an obvious allegiance to one political party. The new prime minister, Suleyman Demirel, is committed to maintaining Turkey's system of parliamentary democracy.

Turkey's government is facing exciting opportunities created by the collapse of the former Soviet Union. About 40 million people in the former Soviet republics are Moslems, speaking a form of Turkish. The Turkish government is developing new policies to respond to these new allegiances.

TURKEY'S PARLIAMENT

The Grand National Assembly consists of two chambers: the National Assembly and the Senate. The National Assembly has 450 members elected for a period of four years. The Senate, on the other hand, has 150 members, plus 40 others who are not elected but appointed as members for life.

The president, who wields the executive power of the state, is elected for a seven-year term.

Above: **Turkey's Parliament House in Ankara is constructed to withstand earthquakes. Inside the building are 16 large chandeliers, representing the 16 states of Turkey.**

PROPORTIONAL REPRESENTATION

Turkey's electoral system elects members of Parliament according to the proportion of votes they attract, rather than simply letting the politician with the most votes win. There is also a system of multi-member constituencies. This means that, instead of having just one politician elected for one seat, there may be three or four members of Parliament elected—reflecting the proportion of votes that each party received.

The traditional argument against proportional representation is that it allows a multitude of minority parties to win seats, and thus weakens the chances of a stable government that has a clear majority of seats being formed. Turkey has modified its version of proportional representation to deal with this. A party needs 10% of the national vote before it can be considered for a seat in Parliament. And a party must win 25% of the vote in a four-seat constituency, 33% in a three-seat constituency, and so on. The result is that three parties dominate Turkey's political life: the Motherland Party, the True Path Party, and the Social Democrat Populist Party.

Left: Parliament in session. The Turkish republic is a parliamentary democracy. Three political parties are currently represented.

Below: The Turkish army has played an important role in preserving the stability of the country.

THE ARMY

The army has intervened in the process of government on three occasions: in 1960, 1971, and 1980. To many observers both inside and outside Turkey, the coup in 1980 was the most justifiable one because of the turmoil that was then tearing the country apart. Before the coup, the country had collapsed into political street fighting that was taking, on average, 15 lives a day.

Each coup has been followed by a voluntary return to parliamentary democracy. It has been said that Turkey is the only country where army coups are designed to protect democracy. The army sees itself as the guardian of the secular reforms introduced by Ataturk, and regards the revival of Islamic fundamentalism with some alarm and trepidation.

The army is more than just a branch of the state. It perceives its role as being a broader one than just carrying out the orders of Parliament. Military service is compulsory. For many conscripts from isolated rural districts, the years spent in the army are an introduction to another way of life.

Turkey possesses a Constitutional Court, whose function is to rule on the constitutional nature of laws passed by Parliament. Normal cases are handled by a Council of State and a Court of Appeals.

HUMAN RIGHTS

There have been serious allegations of violations of human rights in Turkey. Movies and the press are subject to censorship if their social and political criticism is seen as disruptive or offensive. Allegations of torture in prison are routine, and it is claimed that there is a "shoot to kill" policy toward terrorists. It is not uncommon for judges to hand out death sentences for political offenses. The government's treatment of the Kurdish minority has also been the subject of severe criticism.

Such allegations are seen as a stumbling block to Turkey's entry into the European Community (EC). However, the government defends itself by claiming the criticisms refer only to isolated cases, and that attempts are being made to redress such wrongs. Turkey has, for instance, signed international conventions against torture. There is also a draft bill before the National Assembly to commute the death penalty

THE KURDS

The Kurds form a minority in Turkey, making up 7% of the population. Their feelings of persecution have led to an ongoing conflict with the government. The Kurdish Workers' Party, an outlawed group, calls for separation from Turkey.

Kurdish rebels in Turkey are linked to the Kurdish separatist movement in Iraq. Before the 1991 Gulf War, Turkey and Iraq had signed an agreement allowing the armed forces of each country to pursue and attack Kurdish rebels operating on either side of the border. In the aftermath of the Gulf War, when worldwide sympathy was aroused for the Iraqi Kurds who defied Saddam Hussein, Turkey's own treatment of its Kurds came into the limelight once again.

to life-imprisonment for 13 types of crimes. The death penalty has not been carried out since 1984.

The legal system, which critics say is under the control of the government, does not always support the state. At one trial 50 leading writers accused of subversion, because they organized readings of a left-wing poet, were acquitted. At the same time, however, an editor received a 16-month jail sentence after being found guilty of insulting the president.

Moreover, the curtailment of other rights does remain. The laws against trade unions are particularly severe. Unions in many cases are not allowed to strike, engage in political discussions, or even have more than two people picketing at any one workplace.

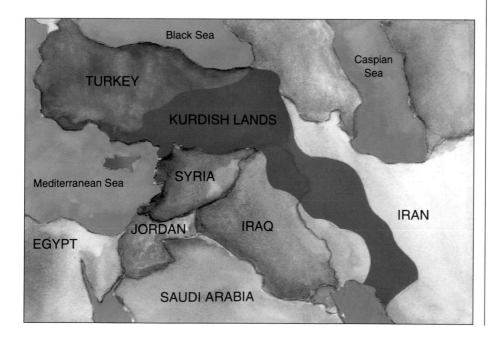

Left: **The Kurds live in an area spread over several countries, including Turkey, Iraq, and Iran.**

ECONOMY

DURING the 1980s, Turkey's economy was in disarray, crippled by debts that it could not pay. Today, however, it has transformed itself into a healthy state that is the envy of its Black Sea neighbors.

The collapse of Soviet power has created a void in the region that Turkey has expanded to fill. Once again, the Istanbul bazaar is as filled with a multitude of races and nationalities as it must have been in the heyday of the Ottoman empire.

Even during the Gulf War, when Turkey's geographic position and Islamic character might have made it seem vulnerable, foreign investment continued. The average per capita income is $2,500. This may be low compared to North American or Western European standards, but Turkey's continual economic growth should allow it to forge ahead.

On the less optimistic side, there are continuing problems for the Turkish economy. A high birth rate contributes to an unemployment problem, and this results in a steady drift of peasants to urban centers in search of work. The cities cannot absorb all the available labor. For many decades, unemployed Turks have gone to countries such as Germany and Sweden to work.

Above: **Cotton is an important commercial crop. Over 60% of the country's cotton output comes from the coastal areas of the Mediterranean region.**

Opposite: **A bumper harvest of red pepper. Turkey's varied climate enables a wide range of fruits and vegetables to be cultivated.**

Members of the Black Sea Economic Cooperation summit pose for a picture. The summit aims, among other things, to bring peace, stability, and prosperity to the Black Sea region.

"It's like what the European Community is for the Europeans. We are on the crossroads and Turkey is at the center."
—The president of Romania, commenting on the cooperation among the Black Sea states in 1992.

NEW LINKS

In June 1992, leaders of 11 countries around the Black Sea met in Istanbul to forge a new economic alliance. Turkey did not just host the Black Sea Economic Cooperation Summit but emerged as the regional leader in this new grouping. Apart from Turkey and Greece, all the participating countries had been under the control of the Soviet Union for 70 years. The new grouping represents a change of direction and a fresh start to economic cooperation.

Business people now flock to Ankara and Istanbul from countries that only a few years ago were small forgotten states in the Soviet Union. Ironically, these countries—Azerbaijan, Armenia, and Georgia—are part of the hinterland of Central Asia from where, a thousand years ago, the great westward Turkish migration began.

The Black Sea union began with the setting up of a regional bank and agreement on the need to work together on the problem of Black Sea pollution. The plan is to work toward an economic union where people, goods, and capital can move freely between the member states.

Turkey is also building strong economic links with the Russian Republic. Trade with Russia stands at $1.8 billion a year. It is likely to increase steadily in the future. Turkey receives essential supplies of natural gas from Russia, and both countries have a mutual interest in promoting economic links.

Turkey has been waiting to join the lucrative European Community (EC) for a number of years. In the first few years after its application in 1987, it seemed unlikely that Turkey could participate equally with the rich nations of the EC. The difference in income levels was just too great.

Despite new links with the Black Sea states, it is a fact of life that membership in the EC would be a tremendous benefit to Turkey's economy. As the economies of the European states come closer and closer together, so does the possibility of Turkey's economy being excluded from this rich club. Turkey continues to wait, joined by countries such as Poland and Hungary. However, it seems likely that Turkey will not become a full member until after the turn of the century.

UNEMPLOYMENT AND MIGRATION

While Turkey's membership application for the EC continues to languish, migrant Turkish workers are employed to clean and refurbish the countless halls and offices of the EC buildings in Brussels. They are just some of the thousands of Turks, known as guest workers, who leave their own country every year to seek employment in Europe.

The cities of Turkey cannot accommodate, let alone employ, the numbers who pour in each year from the countryside. The peasants settle on the fringes of Istanbul and Ankara in quickly built houses called *gece*

Many of the rural unemployed have migrated to the cities to look for jobs. Some, such as these itinerant vendors, eke out a living on the streets.

kondu ("GEDJ-erh KOHN-doo"). Tradition says that if a house can be built in one night, the builders have a right to live there. It is estimated that as much as half the population of Ankara and Istanbul live in *gece kondu* areas.

With overcrowding and unemployment rampant in the cities, Turks have turned westward to the prosperous countries of the EC. Germany is traditionally the first choice for migrant workers. They have to cope with the culture shock of leaving, say, a small village in eastern Anatolia, where they knew everyone, for the harsh anonymity of a construction site in Dusseldorf.

Below and opposite: **Turkey is famous for its handicrafts. Below, a woman weaves a carpet that will eventually find its way into the shops or the export market.**

The only compensation, apart from the wages they receive, is that Turkish communities have developed in many European capitals, and migrants going there know they will not be alone.

In recent years, this practice of migrating to Europe for work has suffered a setback from two quarters. First, a general economic downturn has depressed the economies of countries such as Germany, and Turkish workers now find themselves competing for work with native unemployed labor. Second, the breakup of the Soviet Union has led to a surge of Eastern Europeans flocking to the West in search of work and a new way of life. The combined effect of these two factors has weakened the demand for Turkish workers and lowered the rates of pay.

CRAFTWORK AND THE ECONOMY

Carpet weaving is more than just a craft, as carpets are one of the country's main products. Tourists are attracted to *kilim* ("KIL-aym"), colorful pileless rugs woven on looms in bold patterns that have a variety of uses: on the floor, the bed, or as a wall decoration. The better quality carpets are made with natural dyes.

Copperware is not as common as it once was when, along with a carpet, it was an essential gift for newlyweds. Copperware used to be handmade, but the majority of copper products

now found in the bazaars are machine-made. Nevertheless, there is a long tradition in design work, and many handsome pieces are still being produced and sold.

Leatherwork is another craft that has been practiced for centuries in Turkey. The skin of young animals produces the higher quality items. There are large workshops in Istanbul catering to the domestic and tourist markets.

Meerschaum is an absorbent clay quarried in the west of Anatolia. Turkey is the only country that possesses sufficient reserves to make it commercially viable. It is fashioned into pipes, cigarette holders, and decorative items.

Below: **A farmer on his tractor and an industrial plant. Although Turkey is industrializing rapidly, agriculture still plays a very important role in its economy. Fruit and vegetables, cotton, and tobacco are among the leading sources of income. Turkey's industries are directed mainly toward the processing of agricultural products, metallurgy, textiles, and the manufacture of automobiles and agricultural machinery.**

FARMING

The majority of Turks continue to work on the land. The most important crops are wheat, rice, barley, cotton, tea, tobacco, olives, hazelnuts, and fruit. The tobacco industry is principally based on the Black Sea coast, and the domestic market is just as important as exports abroad.

Vineyards and orchards cover around 10,000 square miles, providing valuable yields of wine, citrus fruit, olives, hazelnuts, and tea for export. The Black Sea coast is especially known for its high concentration of small family estates deriving their income from hazelnuts. Tea is grown in the northeast of the country, where the higher rainfall is a vital factor.

Farmers in Turkey face the problem of fragmented holdings. Farms consist of small lots that are often separated from one another by considerable distances. It was once calculated that 70% of all peasant holdings were in the form of at least four different plots.

INDUSTRY

Despite the importance of agriculture, Turkey is industrializing fast. Istanbul is the focus for 30% of the country's industrial activity, with over 350,000 workers engaged in producing well over half of the land's total industrial output.

Primary sources of employment are in enterprises such as shipbuilding, automobiles, pharmaceuticals, and machine parts. The textile industry is also important,

along with cement and iron and steel works. Coal, chromium, and copper are mined.

Tourism plays an important role in the national economy. The coastal areas, especially around the Mediterranean, attract sun-seekers, while inland, the amazing number of antiquities draws dedicated visitors.

The old stereotype of the Turkish work ethic is an unfavorable one. Commercial virtues such as thrift, efficiency, and productivity were seen as alien to a Turkish mentality unsuited to the rigors of competitive capitalism. This is very much a thing of the past. Modern workers in shipbuilding yards or pharmaceutical plants are just as much prepared to work hard for good wages as their counterparts in other parts of the world.

Tourists explore a Lycian burial ground in one of Turkey's many historic sites. Tourism is a major source of revenue for Turkey.

THE TURKS

DURING THE LONG YEARS of the Ottoman empire, the Turks ruled over a vast area and a disparate collection of races and cultures. Modern Turkey, however, is the kernel of the old empire. It was founded on Anatolia, the traditional home of the Turks when they first arrived from the east in the 11th century. During the period that gave birth to the republic, most ethnic minorities left Turkey, though not always of their own accord. Greece and Turkey were able to exchange their minority populations, but the Armenians suffered a harsher fate. Over 1 million of them perished in the first large-scale genocide of the 20th century. In Turkey today, the Kurds are the only significant ethnic minority. The Laz and Hemsin people are ethnic Turks, but they have a very distinct identity of their own. They live mainly along the eastern coast of the Black Sea.

Today, the Turks are the world's fifth largest ethnic group, with more than 160 million people, when one includes the Turkic states of Central Asia. This makes the Turks a numerically more important group than the Arabs or Russians.

Opposite: **An elderly man from Cappadocia.**

Below: **Two girls from Antalya. The Turks are a mixture of many ethnic groups, including the Hittites, the Greeks, the Persians, and the Seljuk Turks.**

A family from an old part of Ankara, dressed in traditional clothes. Most city dwellers, however, wear Western clothes.

THE TURKS

The Turks have a very mixed heritage. Long before Turkish-speaking people arrived, the land that is now Turkey had been home to many other races and tribes. The Hittites created the first important empire in the area. Later came the Greeks, Persians, and Romans. The Celts and the Jews were there just before the Christian era. In the east and southeast, Kurds and Armenians were prominent. When the Turks finally arrived, they did not expel these peoples but assimilated them instead. The result is that the Turks are a genetic mix of European and Asian. Some Turks are olive skinned with black hair and brown eyes. Others are blond and blue-eyed.

The original homeland of the Turks was in Central and Eastern Asia. The earliest written evidence of their language dates back to the 8th century.

Over the following centuries, the Turks moved westward in search of land and food. By the 12th century, they had occupied Anatolia.

The contemporary citizens of Turkey owe their sense of national identity to the reforms of Kemal Ataturk. It was Ataturk who convinced the Turks to take pride in the new country that emerged after the chaos surrounding the breakup of the Ottoman empire. A proud, nationalistic spirit is still part of the Turkish mentality today.

Turks, at least in Europe, have had a reputation for violence and general disagreeableness. The reason lies in a deep-rooted, historical prejudice. For centuries, the Ottoman empire was the sworn enemy of Christendom and viewed as Europe's number one enemy. The very word "Turk" came to describe anyone whose behavior was unkind or savage. Today, the Turks rank among the friendliest of people. Their sense of hospitality is renowned.

Turkey has 54 million people, and almost half of them live in urban areas. Migration from rural areas to the cities has become a common pattern as the country industrializes.

47

THE LAZ

Turks themselves often refer to anyone living east of Trabzon as "Laz," although this is not strictly true. The Laz people, who number about 100,000, inhabit a particular region of the eastern coast beyond Trabzon as well as certain inland localities. The main Laz towns are Pazar, Ardesen, and Hopa. The Laz people have lived in this part of the country since pre-Christian times, speaking a language close to Georgian.

Laz men are distinguished from Turks by their red hair and sharper features. Their success in business, especially in the shipping industry, has enabled them to lead a comfortable existence. Their expertise in shipping has a long history, going back to the days when they were famous as pirates and skilled boat builders. Today, their love for material things shows itself in a liking for expensive Western clothes. Traditional Laz costumes are rarely seen.

Under the influence of the Byzantine empire, the Laz were Christianized. Later, Islamic conversion came with the Ottomans. However, for quite some time the Laz kept their Christian names along with their new Islamic ones. They even practiced both religions and were known once as "Crypto-Christians." Today, the Laz are nearly all Moslem and fully integrated into the Turkish way of life.

The Laz live by the coast with the Pontic Mountains behind them. Many small rivers flow down to the sea, and the Laz use the surrounding trees to build small bridges, chalets, and *seranders* ("serh-AN-derhs"). Seranders are small buildings erected on sticks to store the corn used for making the

A Turkish woman and her granddaughter. Their Caucasian looks point to their European ancestry.

region's distinctive bread.

The Laz region once had an important Greek community, but most of its members were deported to Greece after World War I. Today, it is becoming increasingly rare to hear Greek spoken.

THE HEMSINLIS

Throughout the Byzantine age, as well as during most of the Ottoman period, a community of Christian Armenians lived as neighbors to the Laz. Eventually, most of these Armenians left or were driven out to the east and into Syria. The Islamic and Turkified Armenians that remained behind were known as *Hemsinlis* ("HEM-shin-lees").

The Hemsinlis share with the Laz Caucasian looks that separate them from the mainstream Turks. They are known for their culinary skills in making pastries and puddings. Many of the prestigious pastry shops of Istanbul and Ankara are owned by people from the Hemsin areas.

Hemsin women have retained some of their traditional costume, especially the scarves that are brightly patterned and often worn as turbans. Strangely enough, the scarf material is not woven in Turkey but comes from India. This may be a throwback to Byzantine days, when nearby Trabzon prospered as a bustling commercial center on the Silk Route.

Like the Laz, the Hemsinlis have access to the forests of oak, beech, birch, maple, and chestnut. They use the wood of these trees to complete the top half of their *yayla* ("YAHR-lah"), dwellings built of stone to half their height and then completed in timber. Constructed in the uplands, most of them are uninhabitable until spring because of the harsh winter climate.

A woman gathers wood from a tea plantation near Trabzon in the Black Sea coastal region.

Below: **A Kurdish man takes his grandson out for a stroll.**

Opposite: **Another Kurd poses with his two wives.**

THE KURDS

The Kurds are an ethnic group living in an area called Kurdistan. They were originally nomads, but the modern states created after World War I left them stateless. Between 1925 and 1938, Turkey was the scene of almost continuous Kurdish uprisings, all of which were brutally put down. At the time, all aspects of Kurdish culture were suppressed: traditions, forms of dress, language. Even the very word "Kurd" was banned and replaced by the euphemisms "Mountain Turk" or "Eastern Turk."

The Kurds live mostly in the southeast of Turkey, and their position continues to be a problematic one. The government of Turkey is reluctant to admit their status as a separate ethnic group. Officially, the Kurds are regarded as part of the Turkish peoples originating in Central Asia. Linguistically, too, their language is regarded as a Turkish dialect and not as a separate language, which helps identify them as the most important ethnic minority in Turkey. There are some 12 million Kurds in Turkey, amounting to almost one in five of the population.

THE TRAGEDY OF THE KURDS

The Kurdish people do not have their own country. They are spread out across Turkey, Iraq, Iran, and the former Soviet Union. The largest number of Kurds is in Turkey. If the Kurds were ever to establish their own country, Kurdistan, it would occupy a mountainous area divided between Turkey, Iran, and Iraq. A small number of Kurds inhabit Syria and Armenia.

Claims for Kurdish autonomy have their basis in a treaty signed shortly after World War I that promised them an independent Kurdistan. On more than one occasion, they have risen in rebellion against the government of Iraq. In 1988, thousands of Kurdish refugees fled to Turkey trying to escape chemical warfare attacks by the Iraqi government. In 1991, following the defeat of Iraq in the Gulf War, it seemed as if they might be successful in achieving autonomy, but this has not happened.

In Turkey, the Kurdish Workers' Party (PKK) has for a number of years conducted a guerrilla war in pursuit of its claims for autonomy. Since 1984, 3,500 people have been killed as part of its armed struggle. In March of 1992, some of the worst violence broke out during celebrations of Nowruz, and about 50 people were killed.

Large numbers have been transferred to eastern Anatolia. But it is not unusual to come across predominantly Kurdish villages in central and even western Turkey.

In recent years, there has been more willingness on the part of the Turkish authorities to acknowledge the Kurdish people. During a recent celebration surrounding Nowruz, the Kurdish New Year, the prime minister accepted a bouquet of flowers from a moderate Kurdish leader in honor of Nowruz. This kind of scene would have been unthinkable at any time during the previous 70 years.

The Kurds have inhabited western Anatolia

since the 7th century A.D. One of their most famous ancestors is Saladin, who has entered the history books as the shrewd and chivalrous opponent of the Christian crusaders.

LIFESTYLE

TURKEY IS A LARGE COUNTRY. Although nearly all Turks follow the same religious beliefs, significant differences in lifestyle exist. The most fundamental difference is that between life in the countryside, where the majority of Turks still live and work, and the urban areas. There are also important differences between the life of a typical Turkish woman and her male counterpart. At the same time, there are certain underlying national characteristics.

NATIONAL PRIDE

Turks are an immensely proud people, not in an arrogant manner or a naive flag-waving way, but in a more personal way. Ataturk is often credited with having created this sense of national identity, although to some extent he also cultivated feelings that were already there.

A famous remark of Ataturk's is a clue to the Turks' self-perception. He gave a speech that included a comparison of Turkey with other countries. He remarked: "So what does it matter if our regime does not resemble democracy, does not resemble socialism, does not resemble

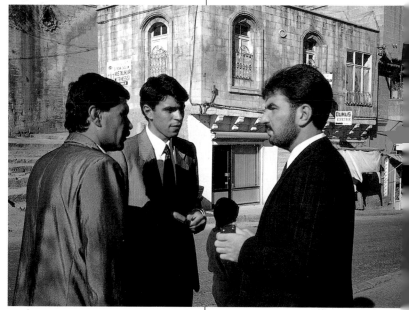

anything? Gentlemen, we should be proud of not resembling anything; because we resemble ourselves!"

This last remark, *Biz bize benzeriz* ("we resemble ourselves"), is obviously true, but it also indicates a belief in one's own special identity. It has been said that a Turk's first duty is to be proud.

"He's a lucky man who can say, 'I am a Turk.'"
—Kemal Ataturk

53

The pride rarely becomes xenophobic (an irrational fear and rejection of foreigners), although there is a longstanding enmity toward Greeks. Strangers are welcomed and made to feel welcome. Tourists making the acquaintance of a Turk are very likely to find themselves invited to their home as privileged guests. Hospitality is taken very seriously by Turks.

THE POSITION OF WOMEN

By tradition, Turkish culture favors the male over the female. To a large extent, this is related to the Islamic religion, for the Koran, the holy book of Moslems, allows for polygamy and male superiority.

Ataturk set out to modernize and secularize a society that was, and still is, both Moslem and traditionally masculine in its prejudices. Ataturk opened high schools, colleges, and the civil service to women.

Ataturk's reforming spirit is still at work, but the position of women has not changed fundamentally. For generations, women have been brought up to be submissive to male authority, not just their father or husband, but any brothers or male in-laws. Despite modern laws that proclaim the equality of the sexes, male superiority is still taken for granted. In rural parts of the country especially, women are rarely seen alone in public places such as restaurants or beaches. After dark, women tend not to go out, not even accompanied, and certainly not alone.

Two Turkish women, in full clothing, take their children for a dip in the sea. Modesty and a strict dress code forbid Turkish women from wearing swimsuits.

Progressive women have organized campaigns in an attempt to raise people's consciousness. In 1989, there was the "purple needle campaign" in Istanbul in which feminists handed out purple-ribboned hat pins to women—to be used in response to male harassment.

Women in Turkey do not commonly wear the veil that is obligatory in neighboring Moslem countries. The wearing of the chador, or veil, was banned by Ataturk as a symbolic gesture. In rural areas, however, a black headpiece is worn by women. It is known as the *charshaf* ("shahr-chAHF"), and can be worn in a very similar way to the veil.

The inferior position of women is reflected in statistics that show that the majority of young people attending junior high school are boys.

Turkish children are the pride and joy of their parents.

CHILDBIRTH

Such is the position of women that, among the more traditionally minded, the birth of a son is far more important than the birth of a daughter. Magical prescriptions and superstitions are associated with childbirth. When they are used, it is often in order to ensure the birth of a male child.

Immediately after the birth of a child, and for the 40 days that follow, tradition says that the child is very vulnerable to the malign influence of witches and devils. One way of trying to protect the newborn is by "salting"—the baby's body is rubbed all over with salt in the belief that this will give the child strength to resist harmful influences. A custom that is no longer as common as it once was involves the placing of a tortoise under the child's pillow at night. It is believed that the tortoise will protect the infant.

The protection of the newborn is related to a more general fear in the "evil eye," or as it is called in Turkey, *nazar* ("naz-AR"), the "look." There is even a tradition of deliberately dressing the infant, for the first 40 days of life, in as unflattering a way as possible. For instance, the clothes could be put on backward in an attempt to deceive the evil eye.

As children grow up, the need to protect them against evil forces does not diminish. Relatives and friends, when they praise a young child, will often add the word *maashallah* ("MAH-SHAH-ahl-lah") as an invocation to God for security. Children themselves wear a blue bead as a talisman, or charm for protection, especially against a blue-eyed person, who reputedly could impart harm through an evil look.

CIRCUMCISION

Every Turkish male, if he is a Moslem, will be circumcised around the age of seven. Sometimes the child will be older than this and the act of circumcision becomes part of an initiation ceremony that marks the change of status from childhood to adulthood.

Among educated, well-off families in the cities, it is becoming increasingly more common for the circumcision to take place in a local private clinic or hospital. Traditionally, the event is a cause for rejoicing, and a celebration party is organized to mark the occasion. The cost of such parties is often shared. Family members and relatives of the young boys consider it an act of piety to contribute toward the expenses.

The act of circumcision traditionally is accompanied by its own rituals. When the doctor performs the act, male friends and relatives clap, and a pistol is sometimes fired to mark the occasion. The child later receives visitors who drop small coins into a handkerchief.

For Turkish males, circumcision is an important event in their lives. The fortitude shown by the boys will reflect on the family reputation.

In Turkish society, male friends greet each other with a great display of affection.

A MALE WORLD

Male relationships based on friendship are common among Turks. It is not uncommon to see two men walking down the street holding hands. When men meet, they often embrace and kiss in a more demonstrative way than women do. Yet homosexuality is not accepted and is certainly not part of the male self-image.

A characteristic virtue is that of honor or *namus* ("NAHM-erhs"). An insult can be viewed as deadly serious and can call for a violent defense. Even today, newspapers still carry reports of murders that have their origin in arguments among men, often starting as a dispute over some seemingly unimportant matter.

The notion of honor is closely related to that of loyalty. An individual's sense of grievance with someone can develop over time into a blood feud between members of rival families. Such feuds can last for generations and periodically break into serious acts of violence and death.

Turkish men like to socialize. The coffee house or small village restaurant is the traditional meeting place for men. Women do not frequent such places. Even the waiters and managers are always men.

FAMILY LIFE

The family is at the heart of Turkish life. The most common form of celebration among family members is a meal, especially if someone has been away for some time. In extended families, respect is accorded first to the oldest male. An aged grandfather will continue to be treated as the highest authority even if all the daily decisions are regularly made by the younger generation. A middle-aged man will still rise to his feet when his father enters a room.

In rural areas, households remain large because of the extended family tradition. There is an unspoken agreement that older members of a family need to be supported. A family consisting of more than seven members is not uncommon.

The high regard that is accorded to the family is best demonstrated during Seker Bayram. It marks the end of the religious month of fasting, and is very much a family affair. Special visits are made to the eldest member of the family, whose hand is ceremoniously kissed as a mark of respect.

WEDDINGS

In cities or towns, a Turkish wedding usually consists of a short ceremony in the city hall. This is followed by a private reception where food and drink is consumed to the accompaniment of music. In the countryside, a marriage is often a far more prolonged affair. To begin with, the marriage itself will have been debated and bargained over for some time. The parents of both parties will meet and discuss the suitability of the match. The old practice of paying a bride price has not completely died out. This was once common throughout the country, and harks back to the time when women were merely a form of chattel that could be bought and sold. Such a practice does not occur in the cities today and is almost unknown in the more advanced Aegean and Black Sea areas. But in remote rural regions in eastern and southeastern Turkey, the tradition lives on.

A marriage ceremony in the country requires more organizing than one in a town does. By tradition, the bride is taken to the bridegroom's house in a procession surrounded by musicians, with the bride raised above the others. Nowadays, the procession is likely to take the form of a cavalcade of cars, jeeps, small buses, and even tractors. The reception afterward tends to be a noisy affair, with dancing and music lasting through the night. A wedding in the countryside is now one of the few occasions when traditional folk dancing is seen performed in national costume.

A characteristic form of entertainment at a wedding in the countryside is communal dancing, but with the men segregated from the women. Each group forms a line, linked by hand, and dances to folk music usually played by a band using traditional instruments.

FUNERALS

As is common throughout the Moslem world, funerals are traditionally attended only by men. The end of life is marked in a quiet and dignified manner. Cemeteries reflect this simple dignity, and there is a marked absence of ostentation. Often a plain piece of stone marks the final resting place. Most families will have a *mevlud* ("mervh-LAHKH") recited as a prayer for the deceased. A mevlud is a poem that celebrates the birth of the Prophet Mohammed.

Coffins lie in front of a mosque waiting for funeral ceremonies.

The simplicity of a Turkish funeral reflects to some extent the fatalism that Islam espouses. The will of Allah (God) is comprehensive and includes the moment of death.

An exception is the grave of a revered holy man. The graves of such men are sometimes treated as places of worship, and people pray at them for special requests. A small animal may even be sacrificed at the spot as an act of thanksgiving.

61

Istanbul is badly over-crowded. With over 250,000 peasants arriving in the city every year, Istanbul has less green space than any other European city: only two square yards per person.

URBAN LIFE

For the educated elite, life in Istanbul or Ankara is as cosmopolitan and easy as it is in most other major European cities. English is commonly spoken and families have domestic servants, often peasant girls from the eastern part of the country.

For the majority of working people in the cities, life can be demanding and uncomfortable. Housing is a problem due to the continuous influx of new residents from the countryside, and the number of gece kondu continues to grow. However, these squatters' dwellings bear little resemblance to their counterparts in Latin American cities, or the inner-city slums in North America. Although they are supposed to be constructed in one night, they are built to last a lot longer. Most are connected to the main electricity supply, and official figures indicate that over 90% of them have television sets and refrigerators.

The overcrowding in the cities and the fact that the majority of working people cannot afford their own cars have caused a severe strain on the public transportation system. One economical solution has been the *dolmus* ("dohl-MERHS"). The word means "stuffed," which gives some indication of their popularity. The dolmus is a car or minibus that travels a set route, picking up passengers and dropping them off along the way. There are no recognized bus stops, and pedestrians simply hail them like a taxi. The fares are only slightly more than the public buses, but during the rush hour they are just as crowded. The standard fare is 15 cents and a monthly pass costs $4.

The growth of the urban population is posing other problems for the authorities. For instance, Izmir, Turkey's third largest city, has a population of 1.9 million, which is increasing at 5% a year. Yet, the city still has no sewage plant, although one is being planned at a cost of $500 million and is supposed to become operational in 1993.

A coeducational school in Istanbul provides elementary schooling. Of the children entering junior high schools, 70% are boys and 30% are girls.

EDUCATION

In theory, education is free to every citizen in Turkey. In practice, there is a marked and far-reaching difference in schooling between the countryside and the cities and towns.

Villages provide elementary education for everyone up to the age of 12, but high schools are not available for every rural community, unlike in the cities. Children over the age of 12 who wish to continue their education usually have to travel long distances. When the school is too far away, the student must board there. Unfortunately, the expense involved may prove too much for poorer families and education effectively comes to an end.

Whether in the urban or rural areas, middle-class families recognize the importance of learning English as a tool for communication and business. If they can afford it, they will send their children to private schools and colleges where English is intensively taught.

The traditional versus the modern: a horse-drawn cart and an engine-driven bus. Animals are still used as a means of transportation, particularly in the countryside.

RURAL LIFE

The most obvious social distinction in Turkey is between the lives of people in the countryside and urban residents. The difference can be seen in nearly all aspects of life and thought. Even the unifying bond of religion is affected by this difference. A visitor to Istanbul or Ankara is not immediately reminded that Turkey is a Moslem country. Alcohol is readily available, for instance, and, superficially at least, women seem to mix with men. In the rural areas of Anatolia, however, the presence of religion is more apparent. Traditional beliefs and practices are still commonplace.

The majority of people in the countryside are peasants earning their living from cash crops such as hazelnuts, tea, and sugar beets. Families are larger and girls marry as young as 14 years of age. Polygamy is illegal according to Turkish law, but it has been a traditional feature of Turkish rural life for centuries. It does not go against customary Islamic beliefs. Even today, polygamy has not completely died out.

THE BAKKAL AND THE BAZAAR

Although supermarkets exist in Turkey, the *bakkal* is still the place where both rural and urban shoppers go for their everyday needs. The bakkal is the traditional small shop that stocks basic foods and beverages. It is nearly always privately owned, and the proprietor is usually behind the counter serving his or her regular customers.

The bazaar, a Persian word meaning market, is found in the main towns throughout Turkey. Bazaars have their origin in Ottoman times, and the concept is basically the same as that behind the modern shopping mall. Various domed buildings are connected to one another by covered arcades, with different parts of the bazaar specializing in certain items. Istanbul has the most famous of all bazaars, claimed to be the largest in the world. In the different sections are found carpets, silver, ceramics, leather goods, pots and pans, and everything else that might be required in the home. Fixed prices are not displayed, but the Turkish shopper will always know what degree of bargaining is required.

The bazaars in Istanbul cater to a wide variety of goods and products, from exquisite jewelry and carpets to every conceivable herb and spice.

RELIGION

Opposite: **A devout Moslem prostrates himself during prayer time. Prayers are said five times a day.**

THE TURKS converted to Islam during the course of their migrations to the West over a thousand years ago. Before their conversion, they were likely influenced by the ancient Chinese worship of a sun god. Traces of this earlier belief system can still be detected today. It is said to explain why farmers in some rural areas beat large drums and shoot off guns to mark an eclipse of the sun.

Today, more than 99% of the country is Moslem.

ISLAM

Islam in Arabic means "submission" to the will of Allah (God). The religion originated in Arabia sometime during the 7th century A.D. through the Prophet Mohammed. The religion asserts that God has sent more than one prophet to earth in order to teach the true way to eternal happiness in the next world. Moses and Jesus were two such prophets who prepared the way for the final revelation of God's word through Mohammed.

Islam divides into two basic groups: the Sunni ("SOON-nee") and the Shiites ("SHEE-aites"). The majority of Turks are Sunni. They follow the Sunna, which is the exemplary practice of Mohammed as recorded in the Hadith ("Hah-DEETH"). The Hadith covers a variety of topics, and acts as a model for correct behavior. As such, it is second only to the Koran in importance.

The Shiites pay particular regard to the Prophet's son-in-law, Ali. The Shiite tradition includes an emphasis on sacrifice and martyrdom. It also believes in a hidden inner meaning to the Koran.

Above: **A Seljuk mosque in Cappadocia. Although Turkey is a Moslem country, it guarantees complete freedom of worship to non-Moslems.**

The most important group of Shiite Turks is the Alevi, a sect whose members mostly live in east and southeast Anatolia. The Alevi are a group divided by religion from the majority of Turks. A social barrier has also developed that is made easier by the fact that the majority of Alevi live in an enclosed area.

A visitor to Turkey is most likely to encounter the presence of Islam by hearing the call to prayer from the muezzin, the Mohammedan crier who proclaims the hours of worship from the minaret of a mosque.

THE KORAN

The Koran, or Qur'an, is to Moslems what the Bible is to Jews and Christians. Moslems believe the book contains the words of Allah as dictated to the Prophet Mohammed in Arabic through the Archangel Gabriel. The Koran is regarded as so holy that any criticism or questioning of it is seen as a sacrilegious act. It is considered by Moslems to be

THE FIVE PILLARS OF ISLAM

The Five Pillars of Islam are duties that every Moslem must perform if he or she is able to do so. They include: (1) a declaration of faith, (2) daily prayers, (3) paying a special tax, (4) fasting, and (5) a pilgrimage.

1. The first pillar, *the shahadah* (declaration of faith), is the deeply felt recital of the creed: "There is no god but God," and "Mohammed is the Messenger of God."
2. The second pillar, the formal prayer to God, must be carried out five times a day at fixed hours, and always said while facing toward Mecca. This is why, in many Turkish hotel rooms, a small arrow on the ceiling indicates the direction of Mecca. Prayer time lasts about 20 minutes and usually occurs at dawn, after midday, in the late afternoon, after sunset, and after dark. It is not unusual to find a small blackboard outside a mosque with the exact times of prayer listed, for they vary slightly according to the time of year.
3. The duty to fast during the month of Ramadan, known as Ramazan in Turkey, constitutes the third pillar.
4. The fourth pillar involves paying a religious tax to help the poor and needy.
5. The fifth and last pillar of Islam is the *hajj*. The *hajj* is the annual pilgrimage to the holy city of Mecca, believed by Moslems to have been built by Abraham (known to Moslems as Ibrahim). Every devout Turk, as a sincere Moslem, hopes to be able to make the pilgrimage at least once during his or her lifetime.

untranslatable, although versions in many other languages have appeared. The revelations that came to Mohammed are grouped into 114 chapters, known as *surahs*. They are not all concerned with matters of doctrine, but touch on many aspects of social life as well.

The Koran is only read in its original Arabic, and a supreme achievement for any Moslem is to learn the entire contents of the book by heart. When the Koran is heard being read on radio or television, it is more of a chant than a straightforward reading. Readers of Arabic point to the incantatory and poetic qualities of the text.

The Koran teaches that God is one and omnipotent. Those who obey God's commands will be judged favorably on the day of resurrection. Those who have sinned will be condemned to eternal damnation through the fires of hell.

THE MOSQUE

The mosque is the Moslem's place of worship. It is usually a fairly simple structure that is basically a hall. Inside the building there is a *mimber*, a kind of pulpit where the imam, or prayer leader, stands. However, it is unlike a pulpit in the sense that no formal sermons are given. Apart from the mimber, the only other essential aspect of the mosque is the *mihrab* ("mi-RABKH"), a prayer niche in the wall showing the direction of Mecca. Outside the mosque, there is usually a minaret from which the call to prayer is made.

Ideally, a Turk will visit a mosque five times a day for the necessary act of prayer. But this is not something prescribed by religious law, and the ordinary Turk will not feel obliged to seek out a mosque a set number of times each day. Unlike Christianity, there is no formal Mass or ritual ceremony associated with the place of worship. In this respect, mosques are not like churches. Another distinction is that Islam does not allow the pictorial representation of Allah. As a result, the interior of a mosque is different from the inside of some churches where pictures or statues are

Mosques vary in size and architectural design, but they have similar parts. Within the mosque itself is an area designed for worship. If it is crowded, an outer courtyard can be used for prayers.

THE PROPHET MOHAMMED

The Prophet of Islam was born into a poor family in Mecca in A.D. 570. When he was 6, his parents died and he was looked after by his relatives until he became a shepherd. As a young man, he earned the title of "al Quraish," meaning the "trustworthy," and married a wealthy widow who at the time was his employer. From 613, he spread the message of his revelations and denounced all forms of idolatry. He never claimed to be more than the messenger of God as he went about Mecca preaching the need for a humble and sober life.

The severity of his attacks on the social life of Mecca's citizens eventually contributed to his decision to flee the city. This secret departure from Mecca is known as the *hegira* ("hi-JI-ra"), after the Arabic word for "the breaking of ties." He established the first Moslem community at Medina, and lived to see his religion return to Mecca when he took the city in 630. He died two years later.

found on the walls. The walls of a mosque may be completely bare.

Worshipers prostrate themselves in prayer with the top of the face touching the floor. Consequently, the floor is always kept as clean as possible and covered with mats or rugs.

In a general sense, Islam is a religion that does not place any special emphasis on ritual or ceremony. The only customary time when Moslems gather is for the Friday midday prayers. Even then, the imam only leads the congregation in prayer.

Ritual ablution, or ceremonial washing, accompanies the five acts of prayer. In larger mosques, an ablution fountain is found in the forecourt of the building. In smaller mosques, it is likely to take the form of a simple tap above a basin in a wall near the entrance.

Shoes are never worn in a mosque. At larger mosques, especially the ones that attract tourists, slippers or overshoes are provided for visitors. Women normally cover their heads before entering, and both sexes refrain from exposing their legs.

Inside a mosque, the words of the first pillar of Islam is found painted or inscribed on the wall: "There is no god but God," and "Mohammed is the Messenger of God." Mosques are often brightly decorated on the outside with strings of colored lights that sometimes spell out concise Koranic messages.

The Ramazan fast is observed annually during the ninth month of the Moslem year. Between the hours of dawn and dusk, a Moslem is forbidden to consume any food or drink. This prohibition also extends to smoking. During Ramazan, newspapers carry details of the exact times of sunrise and sunset.

ATATURK AND RELIGION

Ataturk's aim was to modernize his country and break down some of the cultural barriers that set Turkey apart from the rest of Europe. Inevitably, this meant confronting Islamic beliefs and practices that were seen to inhibit progress. Ataturk did not shy away from the enormity of his task, and set about divorcing religion from the state. Religious education in schools was brought to an end. Even his famous attack on the fez, and its replacement by the European hat, was seen as a symbolic blow to traditional religion. The fez, possessing no brim, facilitated the ritual act of bowing to the ground, whereas a hat would have to be removed before performing the ritual prostration.

More real than symbolic were Ataturk's changes to the legal system of his country. In keeping with traditional religion, the laws of Turkey had followed the rules set down in the Koran. Ataturk removed these laws and replaced them by a legal system borrowed from the West.

Opposite: **Konya's famous green-tiled mausoleum attracts Sufi pilgrims from all over the Middle East.**

THE IMAM

The term "imam" has two different meanings for Moslems. Among Shiites, who are a minority in Turkey as they are throughout the Moslem world, the imam can be a charismatic leader regarded as a supreme source of spiritual authority. In the more general sense, it serves to describe the officiating prayer leader of a mosque who is particularly learned in the traditions of Islam. The religion, unlike Christianity or Judaism, does not possess an institutionalized clergy and the imams are the nearest equivalent. Sometimes they are full-time officials in charge of a mosque. Some are part-time in the sense that they may also have a job outside of the mosque.

MODERN TURKEY AND ISLAM

Turkey is probably the most relaxed Moslem country in the world, with the overwhelming majority of its citizens identifying themselves with Islam. The religious ban on alcohol is commonly disregarded. The national drink is raki, which contains alcohol, and beer is readily drunk. The ban on the eating of pork, however, is strictly observed.

In recent years, the resurgence in Islamic fundamentalism has affected Turkey, though not to the same extent as in some neighboring Moslem countries. At the end of 1989, a law was passed that allowed women to wear head coverings while attending universities. Such a gesture goes against the spirit of Ataturk's secularization of Turkey. Nevertheless, the country remains a non-Islamic state in that it is not governed by Islamic law or administered through Islamic social insitutions.

SUFISM

The popular stereotype of Islam is that of a stern religion that forbids any exuberant display of emotion. Islam is viewed as legalistic in nature, with an emphasis on prohibitions that restrict individual expression. Sufism, a movement within traditional Islam, represents a dramatic contrast to this popular image.

Sufism is a mystical movement that emerged throughout the Islamic world sometime in the 12th century. It stresses the need to relate to God in a personal way. The word comes from *suf,* meaning "wool," because the early storytellers from whom Sufism descended wore clothes made of wool.

Dervishes are Sufis, known for their ecstatic rituals of prayer. Various Sufi sects have their own rituals and observances, but their whirling dances most dramatically distinguish Sufis from mainstream Islam.

Whirling Dervishes. The dancer seeks to achieve a mystical union with God.

THE WHIRLING DERVISHES

Members of the Order of Dervishes seek to attain an ultimate state of mystical communion with God. Music is provided by drums, flutes, and stringed instruments. The dancer is dressed in a jacket over a white robe that reaches to the ankles and flares out as the dance gathers momentum.

Throughout the dance, the right arm is held up to the sky, with the left arm pointing downward. The significance of this is that it represents the way in which grace comes from God and is passed down to people on earth. As the dancers turn and whirl, they repeat a chant under their breath. The musicians also sing a hymn that extols the virtues of seeking a mystical union with God. The dance itself has three clearly defined stages: knowledge of God, awareness of God, and union with God.

Traditionally, a white cone-shaped hat made from camel's hair is worn. This is taken to represent a tombstone and, hence, death. The jacket represents the tomb. During the course of the dance, the jacket is taken off and thrown aside. This symbolizes the casting away of mere earthly existence. The music is seen as the music of the heavenly spheres, and the revolving, dancing figures come to represent the heavenly bodies themselves. That is why the dancers always rotate in a counterclockwise motion. A Sufi poet has tried to express the philosophy behind the dance.

> The truth we have not found,
> So, dancing, we beat the ground.
> Is dancing reproved in me,
> Who wander distraught for Thee?
> In Thy valley we go round,
> And therefore we beat the ground.
>
> — *Yahya Ibn Muadh, Sufi poet*

At the time of Ataturk's reforms, the Order of Dervishes came under attack as a typical example of the outmoded religious beliefs that were seen to hold back the development of a new and modern Turkey. A law was passed and enforced that made it illegal for anyone to wear religious dress in public. This effectively outlawed the Whirling Dervishes and the movement went underground.

Today, a performance of the dance is officially allowed in Konya during the annual Mevlana Festival. The dancers are not only Turks but include Sufi adherents from neighboring Moslem countries as well. The festival commemorates the anniversary of the death of the well-known Sufi poet Celaleddin ar-Rumi on December 17, 1273. Better known as the Mevlana, ar-Rumi founded the sect of the Whirling Dervishes.

The town of Konya has become the center of Sufic mysticism in the Middle East. Within Turkey, it has a reputation as a place of religious zeal and conservatism. This is ironic in a way because the teachings of the Mevlana are more attractive to Westerners than probably any other aspect of Islam.

A portrait of the Mevlana in the museum in Konya.

THE MEVLANA OF KONYA

Celaleddin ar-Rumi was a Persian born in 1207 in what is now Afghanistan. His father was a famous theologian who was invited by the Turkish sultan to Konya in central Anatolia. Ar-Rumi grew up in Konya and developed his own religious philosophy while never abandoning the basic tenets of Islam. His work earned him the prestigious title of the Mevlana.

Ar-Rumi preached the need for a universal and nonsectarian form of divine love. He criticized slavery and the practice of polygamy, and urged a more egalitarian role for women in many aspects of life. Humility was valued as a way of reaching truth. The most dramatic departure from orthodox Islam was in the promotion of dance and music as a means to perceive beauty and achieve union with God.

The town of Konya is the repository of the original illuminated *Mathnawi*, the poetical work of Ar-Rumi. It has been translated into 12 languages. The museum in Konya also contains many of the priceless gifts received by Ar-Rumi during his own lifetime. One of the most famous is a 500-year-old carpet woven from silk. It is supposed to have taken five years to weave and was presented to the Mevlana as a gift from Persia.

"Come, come whoever you are, whether you be fire worshipers, idolaters, or pagans.
Ours is not the dwelling place of despair. All who enter will receive a welcome."
–Celaleddin ar-Rumi, the Mevlana.

MAGIC

The belief in magic predates the conversion to Islam. Vestiges of the belief in supernatural powers can still be found in Turkey today. In the countryside of Anatolia, various small acts are designed to ensure a plentiful supply of water. A scorpion may be pinned to a tree or, more bizarrely, a prayer is attached to the head of a dog and then the creature is thrown into the water.

Good magic is associated with blue beads, and it is common to see a string of blue beads hanging inside trucks and buses. An attempt to secure good fortune is sometimes sought by carrying a magical charm, a *muska*. This often takes the form of a small piece of paper with words from the Koran inscribed in tiny handwriting.

Opposite: **The poetical work of Celaleddin ar-Rumi.**

Left: **Every town in Turkey has at least one mosque, and Istanbul is especially famous for its Blue Mosque. The mosque took its name from the blue Iznik tiles of its interior. Work on the construction of this imposing building began in 1609 and took seven years to complete.**

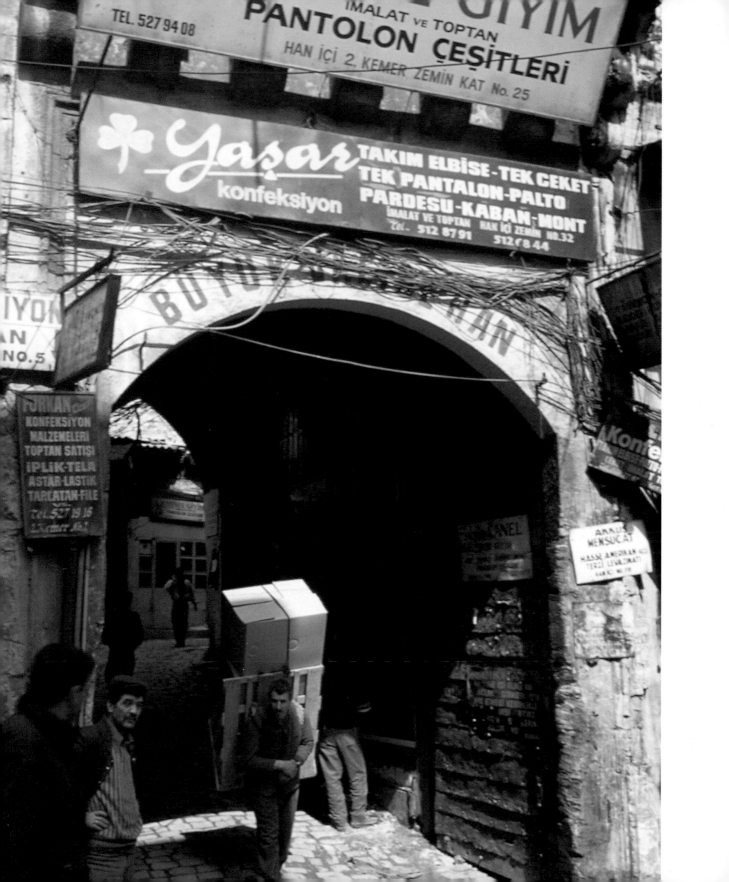

LANGUAGE

TURKEY has never been an isolated culture, so it should come as no surprise that the language has been influenced by different linguistic factors. Although Turkish is not an Indo-European language, it is not a particularly difficult language to learn. The spelling is basically phonetic, meaning fixed symbols always represent the same sound. The English language, by contrast, is notoriously "unphonetic."

ALTAIC AND URALIC

Altaic and Uralic are the names of two different language families that best describe the nature and history of the Turkish language.

Altaic ("al-TAY-ik") is a family of some 40 languages of which Turkish is numerically the largest and most important. Other Altaic languages are Mongolian and Manchu. Manchu was once the common language between China and the outside world, and it may have been a form of this language that the Turks brought with them when they moved West.

Opposite: **Shop signs and addresses in Turkish cover the walls of an old archway in Istanbul.**

Below: **Students learn Turkish in school. Written with Roman characters, Turkish is spoken by some 150 million people in the world.**

Today, Manchu is in danger of extinction. It is only spoken by a minority of the Chinese who live in Manchuria.

Resemblances have also been found with Uralic languages such as Finnish and Hungarian. Similar to these languages, Turkish is based on a set of basic root words that have suffixes added in order to define the meaning more precisely. The Uralic languages have been traced back to a region in the Ural mountains in the former Soviet Union.

THE ARABIC CONNECTION

Turkish has been deeply affected by its exposure to the neighboring languages, Persian (Iranian) and Arabic. This was especially so during the Ottoman period. Indeed, for over a thousand years, Turkish was written using the Arabic alphabet. When Ataturk was radically reforming his country, one of his most audacious moves was to have the Arabic script replaced by the Latin alphabet. This happened in 1928, and Ataturk himself traveled across the country explaining and teaching the new alphabet.

At the time, the change caused some controversy and consternation. This was more to do with religious reasons than anything else. The Koran was written in Arabic, and it is

claimed to be untranslatable. Abandoning the Arabic script was seen as a weakening of this close tie with the source of the country's religion and culture.

Ataturk also set about purging the language of many of its Arabic and Persian words. Because of the common Arabic script, thousands of Arabic and Persian words had found their way into the Turkish language. Ataturk had many of these words replaced by Turkish words. Sometimes, however, the new Turkish words bore an obvious resemblance to European equivalents. The Turkish word for school, for instance, became *okul* from the French *école*. The word for honor became *onur*.

TURKISH PHRASES

There is more than one way of saying "thank you" in Turkish. *Sagol* ("sa-ol") and *tesekkur ederim* are Turkish, but a third acceptable form is clearly French in origin—*mersi*. The influence of French is also shown by the common use of *pardon* to mean "excuse me" when, say, negotiating your way through a crowd of people.

There is also more than one way of saying "no." The word *hayir* means "no," but the word *yok* is more likely to be heard. It literally means "there is none," and is used as an emphatic negative.

When Ataturk was reforming the language in the late 1920s, he also introduced the European titles of Mr. and Mrs. which became, in Turkish, *Bey* (Mr.) and *Hanim* (Mrs.).

Kemal Ataturk giving a lesson in the new alphabet in a public park.

82

MINORITY LANGUAGES

Turkish is spoken by well over 90% of the population. The only significant minority language is Kurdish.

Arabic is the other minority language spoken by as little as 1% of the population. It is only likely to be heard in parts of southeastern Turkey that border Syria.

In the larger cities, Greek and Armenian are sometimes heard. More common, however, would be English or French. The *Turkish Daily News* is printed in English, and the news is read in English, French, and German on the national radio network.

TURKISH VIA SATELLITE

Some 40 million people in what were until recently Soviet republics are Moslems who speak a form of Turkish. Since the breakup of the Soviet Union, Turkey has attempted to communicate with these people through a new television channel known as *Avrasya*, which translates as "Eurasia." Two satellites broadcast this new channel that reaches out to an audience of some 100 million people.

For the last 50 years, these Turkish-speaking Moslems have had little contact with mainstream Turkish life and language. It is estimated that they understand about 70% of the Turkish language. As the new television channel will mainly use Turkish, this will have the effect of bringing together all Turkish speakers.

"It will reach from the Atlantic to the Pacific. It will play a vital role from arts to economics. Culturally speaking, it's going to be a miracle."
—A spokesperson from Turkish Television speaking about Avrasya.

NEWSPAPERS AND TELEVISION

It has been estimated that there are nearly 800 different newspapers and magazines available to the Turkish citizen. This is even more amazing in that, until the middle of the 19th century, no newspapers or magazines were allowed into the country. Of the many hundreds available, however, a high proportion of them are scurrilous and ribald, with illustrations being more important than language.

The most highly regarded national newspaper, both within Turkey and internationally, is the *Cumhuriyet* (*Republic*). This is a mildly left-wing newspaper. There are other popular papers that present more right-wing views.

Both television and radio are under the control of the government, although the advent of satellites is beginning to change this state monopoly. Programs that are imported from the United States and Europe are nearly always dubbed into Turkish. There are, however, regular English-language news programs on TRT2 (Turkish Radio and Television).

ARTS

TURKEY HAS A RICH artistic culture in the fields of art, music, and literature. Most of it is relatively unknown outside of Turkey, although the rich architectural heritage is appreciated by most visitors and tourists. More recently, the most exciting art forms have been movies and novels.

Islam forbids the pictorial representation of the human form. For a country like Turkey that has been Islamic for centuries, this has inevitably influenced the development of art forms. Artists have turned their attention not to the representation of human forms, but to abstract designs and floral motifs.

CERAMIC ART

Ceramics is one of Turkey's oldest art forms. In 1541, Sultan Selim I imported potters from Persia and set them to work in Iznik. There was already a pottery tradition in the town, and Selim's impetus firmly established the potters of Iznik as the supreme practitioners of their art.

By the beginning of the 17th century, over 300 kilns were operating and the tiles produced there were distributed throughout the Ottoman empire. These tiles can still be found decorating some of the finest mosques in Turkey. By 1750, Iznik had declined in importance, and a neighboring town started turning out inferior substitutes. Today, only genuine Iznik tiles are seen as works of art. The most outstanding examples can be seen in the famous Blue Mosque in Istanbul and the Green Mosque in Bursa.

Opposite: **The magnificent ceiling and pillars of a pavilion in the Topkapi Palace.**

Below: **A ceramic tile plate is embellished with snake and floral motifs.**

Below: **A craftsman puts the finishing touches to his musical instrument.**

Opposite top and bottom: **The *ud,* a lute instrument, and the *ney,* a bamboo flute, were both once used by the Mevlana mystic sect.**

MUSIC

It is not difficult to hear music in Turkey, and popular commercial music is as ubiquitous as its equivalent in North America. Turkish music can sound discordant and somber to a visitor hearing it for the first time or listening to it in a tavern in Istanbul.

Until recently, folk music was not written down, and the traditions were kept alive by troubadours. *Ozan,* the folk music of Anatolia, is associated with the *asiks,* folk poets whose name translates as "the ones in love." They accompany their poetry with music played on the *saz,* a flute with a long neck and three sets of strings. Distinct from folk music is the Ottoman military music played with kettledrums, clarinets, cymbals, and bells.

MEVLEVI MUSIC

Earlier, in the Religion chapter, the Mevlana was introduced in connection with the sect of the Whirling Dervishes that he founded. The Mevlana influenced the music of Turkey in a creative and imaginative way because his call for a more personal relationship with God encouraged artistic expression. Members of the Order of Dervishes are called the Mevlevi and their distinctive music is known as Mevlevi music.

An essential part of the dervish dance is music. Mevlevi devotees composed their own music to accompany the ritual of the dance. Indeed, these musical compositions rank as works of art, and can be found in the works of composers such as Kocek Dervis Mustafa Dede (17th century), Dede Efendi (19th century), and Rauf Yekta (early 20th century). The music

STRING INSTRUMENTS

Kemençe This resembles a fiddle, with an oblong body and short neck. The instrument is held vertically and the three strings played with a nylon bow.

Ud This is a lute without a fret, the bar or ridge that is often found on stringed instruments to position the fingers for required notes. The *ud* is very similar to the *oud,* which plays an important role in Arab music.

WIND INSTRUMENTS

Tulum This is a bagpipe found mainly in the eastern part of Turkey that borders on former Soviet territory. There are five finger holes for each of the two pipes that protrude from the goatskin bag. The bag is filled with air by the player through a blowpipe or bellows so that the air passes through the pipes.

Mey This instrument, a metal or plastic rod, resembles an oboe with a large reed, the vibration of which produces the sound as air is pushed through. The same instrument is called *duduk* in eastern Turkey.

PERCUSSION INSTRUMENTS

Davul The davul is a large drum with two sides. Each side is played with a stick of a different length to produce different sounds.

Kasik This is a set of spoons, made either from wood or metal. It is played by dexterous hand movements that bring the faces of the spoons together.

is soothing and relaxing. Modern recordings are available on cassettes and compact discs.

Two of the most traditional Mevlevi instruments are the *ney* and the *kudum.* The ney is a bamboo flute with six finger holes at the front and one thumbhole at the back. It is not an easy instrument to master, and skilled ney players are highly regarded. The other instrument, the kudum, is a small kettledrum. It is usually played in pairs.

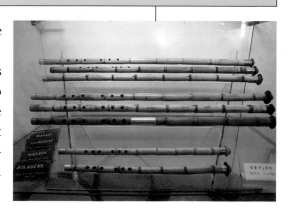

A glove puppet, one of the many types of puppets in Turkey.

PUPPET SHOWS

The shadow puppets of Karagoz and Hacivat are part of a traditional Turkish art form that was once a popular entertainment. It is now in danger of dying out. Karagoz and Hacivat are bearded clown figures whose conversation often acts as a form of social and political comment.

The origin of these two characters is lost in legend. One popular account is that Karagoz was a blacksmith and Hacivat a stonemason, both employed by the sultan Osman in medieval times in the construction of a mosque. Their humorous conversations were so interesting that other workers stopped their work to listen. This incensed the sultan, who had them put to death, only to deeply regret the deed later. He was comforted by establishing a shadow-puppet show of the two men.

A performance of a shadow-puppet show, often just called a Karagoz, consists of three parts. It starts in a Punch-and-Judy fashion with Hacivat being ridiculed by his colleague for speaking fine nonsense. This leads into the second part, where the puppet master displays his or her skill in manipulating the figures through improvisation. The conversation is also improvised as the humor becomes exaggerated. The concluding part of the show depends on the actual play chosen for a particular performance. In *The Treasure Hunt*, for example, a minor character discovers a treasure in a well. But when Karagoz searches in the same place, he only comes up with a crab, a dead mouse, and a bucket with holes in it.

Today, the most common reminder of this art form is found in the marionettes made in the likeness of the two characters. The figure of Karagoz is easy to recognize. He is always hunched and dressed in a brightly colored traditional Turkish costume with a turban on his head. Jointed pieces allow the turban to be flicked back, revealing his bald head. Another jointed piece allows his hand to stroke his beard. Marionettes of

Hacivat portray him as a more serious fellow who strokes his curved beard and is dressed in bright colors.

The better quality puppets are made with the same care that went into the crafting of the figures used in the shadow-puppet shows of the past. They are shaped from camel skin and then stretched over a frame of thin wooden strips. Constant polishing and rubbing reduces the finish to a thin translucent surface that is then colored in the bright red, green, blue, orange, and yellow of Ottoman period costume.

A tile with figures of Hacivat and Karagoz. Karagoz is often portrayed as the merry fellow, and Hacivat the prudent philosopher.

A contemporary Turkish movie. Turkish movies explore issues that go to the heart of Turkish society. Subjects such as generational conflicts, arranged marriages, and the erosion of traditional values are common themes.

TURKISH CINEMA

Turkish cinema came to the world's attention in the 1970s through the internationally famous works of Yilmaz Guney. Guney was imprisoned in the early 1970s following a military coup, but he began directing movies from his prison cell. He would write a script behind bars and give detailed instructions to other movie directors, who then made the movie accordingly. Strangely enough, the movies he made from prison are regarded as his best work. A common theme in his work is the dislocation of rural life brought about by the growth of cities.

His most famous movie is *Yol* (*The Road*). It traces the fortunes of five prisoners who are released from prison on a week's parole. Their behavior becomes a parable of life in modern Turkey and is critical of the way society expects people to behave. Before the movie was released in 1982, Guney escaped from prison and fled to France, where he edited the film.

His last movie, *Duvar* (*The Wall*), also dealt with prisoners and served as a way of criticizing authoritarianism in society at large. Guney died of cancer in 1984 at the age of 46.

Interesting and exciting Turkish movies continued to be made by other moviemakers after Guney's death. Movies have explored the position of women, the misuse of censorship, and the more widespread political oppression that is seen to permeate Turkish society.

TURKISH WRITERS

Yasar Kemal is Turkey's most famous writer. He was born in 1922 and began his writing career by publishing stories of rural life in Anatolia. His works have been translated into English. His more recent ones, such as *Saga of a Seagull* and *The Sea-Crossed Fisherman*, are concerned with the plight of the individual in the modern world.

Other writers, like many of the country's moviemakers, concern themselves with themes that are often considered sensitive and political in Turkey. Irfan Orga (1908-1970), who came to Britain during World War II, was never allowed to return to Turkey. His most famous and successful work was a series of memoirs based on his early life. A typical episode from his work describes the moment when a young woman decides she will no longer wear the veil. Despite the objections of her mother, the woman leaves her house and walks to the village without a veil. Children throw stones at her and she is called all sorts of names, but she perseveres and insists on asserting her own right to dress as she chooses.

The writer who has suffered most for his political beliefs is Nazim Hikmet. He was imprisoned on more than one occasion and fled the country in 1950, never to return. But he continued to write his poetry and called for a socialist solution to Turkey's economic and social problems.

Yasar Kemal, Turkey's foremost literary son.

The Suleimaniye Mosque is considered the most beautiful of all imperial mosques in Istanbul. Built between 1550 and 1557 by Mimar Sinan, it contains the tombs of Suleiman the Magnificent and his wife.

ART AND ARCHITECTURE

It is for its architectural features that Turkey is most admired. The most celebrated architect of the Ottoman period was Mimar Sinan (1489-1588), who designed the Suleimaniye Mosque in Istanbul and many others.

SULEIMANIYE MOSQUE The buildings in this magnificent mosque complex dominate Istanbul's skyline. Before the mosque itself is an elegant courtyard with columns of porphyry (a hard rock with white and red crystals), marble, and granite. There are four minarets: two on the east side with three balconies each, and two shorter ones on the west side with two balconies each. The number of minarets corresponds to the fact that Suleiman was the fourth sultan. The combined number of balconies also has significance in that the sultan was the 10th in line from Osman, the first Ottoman ruler.

The mosque itself, in accordance with traditional Islamic practice, lies beneath a grand central dome. It has a strict geometric design. Its height of 174 feet is exactly twice its diameter, and surmounts a square of exactly 87 feet. There are all together 200 windows. Of these, 138 are of stained glass, designed by an artist

MIMAR SINAN

As a young man, Sinan served in the Ottoman empire and had the opportunity to travel extensively through Eastern Europe and the Middle East. This not only opened his eyes to Islamic art but also the architecture of Christian lands, and he was able to absorb the best of both styles.

He first came to the attention of the sultan when his skill in designing military hardware such as bridges, siege machinery, and ships was recognized. He was appointed as chief architect to Suleiman the Magnificent. Based in Istanbul, Sinan was responsible for a number of small works before embarking on more ambitious projects that have earned him lasting fame. At the height of his fame, he traveled to Mecca and supervised the restoration of the Harem-i-Serif Mosque.

The Aya Sofya (Saint Sophia). This ancient basilica, built by Constantine the Great and reconstructed by Justinian in the 6th century, is one of the architectural marvels of all time.

known as Ibrahim the Drunkard.

The mosque also features another aspect of traditional Turkish art—calligraphy. Calligraphy is the art of penmanship, writing at its most formal and ornamental. It has been a major form of artistic expression in Turkey, East Asia, and Arabic-speaking countries for centuries. Calligraphic inscriptions in Turkish mosques are written in Arabic script with elaborate decorations called arabesque.

AYA SOFYA The Aya Sofya is another of Istanbul's artistic masterpieces. For nearly a thousand years, it remained the largest enclosed space in the world, an incredible achievement considering the fact that the building was commissioned in the 6th century. To construct a dome spanning 105 feet that was not supported by solid walls on four sides was ambitious and audacious. It can be compared with the engineering skill and religious devotion that went into the building of the great medieval cathedrals across Europe.

The interior of the Aya Sofya is a curious mixture of fine Byzantine mosaics and striking calligraphy plates in the old Arabic script. Built as a church, Aya Sofya was later converted into a mosque.

Aya Sofya was built as a church, the Church of the Divine Wisdom, and later converted into a mosque. Sultan Mehmed II had a minaret erected on the southeast corner, and later sultans added three more.

Aya Sofya functioned as a mosque until 1932, when Kemal Ataturk closed it down and turned it into a museum. Periodic calls for its conversion back to a mosque have been resisted. The visitor, however, is reminded of its Islamic past by the large medallions with calligraphic inscriptions of Allah, Mohammed, and the first four caliphs.

TOPKAPI PALACE The mosques of Istanbul may signify the spiritual heart of Turkey, but Topkapi Palace represents the political power of the Ottoman state. It shows the same boldness of conception and marshaling of artistic and engineering talent that went into the religious buildings.

Following a tradition of Islamic architecture, the palace is constructed around a series of buildings surrounded by a number of courtyards. Work began in the mid-15th century on the first of four main courts. The first one

Art and Architecture

was open to the public as a general service area, while the second one was reserved for state functions. The third court was given over to administration and bureaucracy and contained a school for the training of civil servants. The last court, surrounded by flowers, was for relaxation and pleasure.

The harem of Topkapi Palace is not, architecturally, the most important part, but it is certainly the building that attracts most visitors. It consists of 250 rooms. During the reign of Suleiman the Magnificent, there were 1,000 women living there. In 1908, following a revolution, the harem was broken up, and relatives of the slaves were invited to reclaim their kin and return them to their villages.

In Topkapi Palace, there are many priceless art objects from the Ottoman period. The Topkapi dagger is famed for its three very large emeralds, one of which conceals a small watch. The palace also contains a valuable collection of paintings and miniatures dating from the reign of Suleiman to Murat III. Sultans commissioned artists to illustrate their achievements, and these paintings are notable for their depiction of human figures, quite unusual in Islamic art.

LEISURE

TURKS realize the importance of leisure, and there is a strong tradition in the country of slowing down the pace of life and enjoying oneself. There are organized leisure activities, especially sports. In the home, television is becoming increasingly popular as a source of relaxation and leisure.

Traditional forms of leisure include storytelling, greased wrestling, and a visit to a steam bath.

HAMAMS

A *hamam* ("hahm-AHM") is a Turkish steam bath. It is very much a part of Turkish culture. Used by both men and women as a form of relaxation and for personal hygiene, hamams are found in every town in the country. Sometimes they will serve both sexes on different days of the week, and a schedule is posted outside informing the public which days are designated for men and which for women. Larger towns will have separate hamams for men and women. Traditionally, hamams are heated by large wood-burning stoves.

Hamams bear some resemblance to swimming pools. Lockers are provided for personal items, and there is a fixed entrance fee.

Opposite and above: **Whether it is sitting around a sidewalk in convivial fellowship or playing a game of cards in the teahouse, Turks enjoy a relaxed lifestyle.**

A visitor to a hamam usually brings his or her own soap and shampoo. Men also bring their own shaving gear. Instead of a bathing suit, however, the hamam provides a wraparound towel worn as a sarong by the men. Wooden clogs are provided, as well as a regular towel for drying off after the bath.

The central bath chamber is often very ornate. It is usually made of marble, and the numerous sets of basin and taps may be decorated with colored tiles of various designs. A visitor uses a separate basin and, in the case of men, there is a separate area designated for shaving after the main bath.

What makes a hamam different from a regular bath is the sauna-like *gobek tasi* (the "naval stone"). This is a horizontal platform that is invariably positioned above the stoves. Consequently, it is the hottest part of the room, and visitors lay here to absorb the hot vapors. This is also the area where a massage is administered. The Turkish masseur or masseuse has a reputation for delivering a vigorous massage.

SIMPLE PLEASURES

Turks have not lost the art of being able to relax without recourse to highly organized activities or electronic media. In any large town, and this includes Istanbul and Ankara, it is not uncommon to see a group of people walking slowly along the road or sidewalk. Their actual destination is not the purpose of the walk. The object is simply to enjoy each other's company in an informal way, and chat about whatever subject comes into the conversation. A Sunday afternoon is often spent in this manner.

Even the smallest Turkish village will have its coffeehouse where men can talk, sip coffee, and play the national game of backgammon. For many Turkish men, it is a good way of whiling away an afternoon.

Conversing over a cup of coffee is a more specifically male form of leisure. Apart from modern cafés in the big cities that are frequented by both men and women, it is not common for women to socialize in this way. Men, however, will sit for hours over coffee at a small table. Often, there is a game of backgammon in progress, or a pack of cards will be made available by the proprietor. It is still possible to see men seated in a coffeehouse smoking their hubble-bubble pipes. These pipes, known as *nargile*, are often bought by tourists as souvenirs. To use them properly, it is necessary to use compressed Persian tobacco and live coals that are dropped into the brazier end. A single match applied to regular pipe tobacco will never produce the constant flow of smoke that is so contentedly puffed by coffeehouse patrons.

BACKGAMMON

Backgammon has its roots deep in Turkish culture. It was introduced to Britain by the Crusaders, who learned the game from the Turks. Known as *tavla* in Turkey, it is the country's most commonly played game. A backgammon set is easily purchased in almost any town. A set made from wood costs only a few dollars, but it is possible to pay $100 or more for a set made of ivory and inlaid mother-of-pearl.

The game is played by two players, each of whom has 15 flat, round pieces that are moved across the table after each throw of the dice. The backgammon board is composed of two halves: the inner table and outer table. The object of the game is to move your own pieces around the board and home to your own inner table.

STORYTELLING

Turkey has a rich oral tradition with stories and legends passed down from generation to generation. The origin of some of these tales goes back to the ancient days before the Turkish people arrived in what is now Turkey. Then, the Turks were a nomadic race traveling westward from their homes in Central Asia. Although no written records survive of those times, it seems clear from some of the folktales that it was a violent age. The hero of many of these stories is Dedeh Korkut and his band of loyal fighters. The legendary stories, which are still passed on to Turkish schoolchildren in books, comics, and storytelling sessions, recount the heroic deeds of Dedeh Korkut against villains and thieves. In fact, most legends that are passed down in an oral tradition have some basis. It is likely, although it can never be definitely established, that the myths surrounding Dedeh Korkut are based on the real-life exploits of a particularly daring band of Turks who wandered westward from Central Asia.

Even better known than Dedeh Korkut is Nasreddin Hoca. The exploits of Hoca are well known to nearly every Turk, and they have become a cornerstone of Turkish wit and wisdom. Hoca was a 13th-century clown who was able to defeat his opponents not with violence but through his wit and sharp intelligence. Like the traditional court jester, he was able to get away with remarks that would normally get the

The exploits of Nasreddin Hoca, a 13th-century humorist and sage, are legendary. Among the more interesting stories is the one involving Hoca and the cooking pot.

ordinary citizen into trouble.

In one story, he serves a Tartar conqueror who cries aloud because he has caught sight of his own ugly face in a mirror. Hoca joins in the crying but continues to do so even after the Tartar has stopped. When asked to explain, Hoca says, "If you, O great master, can cry for over an hour because you only catch a glimpse of your face in a mirror, then think of poor me who has to see your face every day." Another often repeated story tells of the time Hoca was talking with a friend about the creation of life. Hoca speculates that it would have been better if horses had wings because, then, they would be far more useful to people. Just then, some pigeon droppings fall on his turban. Hoca thinks for a moment and then says, "Allah knows best!"

HOCA AND THE COOKING POT

One day, Hoca called at the house of one of his neighbors. He had a request to make.

"Could you please lend me one of your cooking pots? Mine is broken and needs to be repaired."

"Certainly," said his neighbor, who was pleased to hand over one of his biggest and best pots.

The following day, Hoca returned to his neighbor's house. When the door was opened, the neighbor was happy to see that the pot was being returned to him. Much to his surprise, there was another smaller pot inside the big one.

"Hoca, whose pot is this? You only borrowed my big pot. Where on earth did this small one come from?"

"Ah," replied Hoca in a matter-of-fact tone, "I forgot to tell you that while the big pot was in my house, it had a baby."

The neighbor was expecting to see Hoca smile, but he seemed quite serious. The neighbor decided to adopt a similar tone and replied that the news was unexpected but welcome.

Some time passed and nothing more was ever said on the subject. Then a time came when Hoca called once more at his neighbor's house and asked to borrow a cooking pot. Again, the pot was willingly given to him. This time, however, Hoca did not return to the house. After a while, the neighbor grew anxious and, eventually, decided to call on Hoca himself and ask for the return of the pot. Much to his surprise, Hoca politely informed him that he no longer had the pot.

"What?" said the concerned man. "Are you saying you have lost my best pot?"

"No, I would not be so careless as to lose your best pot. I am afraid something very unfortunate has happened."

"What has happened to my pot?" demanded the neighbor, who was beginning to feel aggrieved.

"Your pot became seriously ill and died, I am afraid to say," replied Hoca in his most serious tone of voice.

"Died! My pot has died, you say. What do you take me for? A fool? Do you seriously expect me to believe that my cooking pot is dead?"

Hoca looked him in the eyes and replied, "Well, you were quite ready to accept that your pot had a baby, weren't you? So what is so difficult about believing that it is now dead?"

SOCCER

This is the most popular sport in Turkey. Any town that can manage it will have its own team, which will be enthusiastically supported at all its matches. Sadly, as is the case with soccer supporters in other parts of Europe, the enthusiasm is often accompanied by outbreaks of violence. Not only do fans attack each other but losing teams are sometimes set upon by their own vociferous supporters. A winning team's supporters are easily recognized; they are often heard before being seen. Constant honking of car horns is a characteristic sign of victory.

Soccer is associated with gambling on a national scale. It is not confined to just local matches, but has been organized into a system that attracts people across the country. Because large sums of money are involved, there have been cases of bribery involving players and managers attempting to fix the result of a league game.

Soccer matches are played over the weekend between September and May, and attract large crowds throughout the country.

Despite the phenomenal interest in soccer, Turkey has not yet achieved any success in the European or world championships. This may have something to do with the fact that each team is allowed to employ only two foreign players.

Greased wrestling is the Turkish national sport. Wrestling has an unbroken tradition in Turkey that dates back to the classical times of the Olympic Games.

GREASED WRESTLING

Wrestling has been a popular sport among Turkish men for centuries. The country is nearly always able to enter a team in the Olympic Games. A special form of wrestling in Turkey that has not yet found its way into the Olympic Games is greased wrestling. Contestants are dressed only in tight leather breeches called *kisbet*. Their bare bodies are rubbed with diluted olive oil. This makes it far more difficult to maintain a hold on one's opponent.

Contestants in greased wrestling are categorized by height and not weight. Competitive matches follow strict rules and are usually introduced by a master of ceremonies, invariably a former champion of the sport. The referee's task is to watch carefully for any illegal move. The actual duration of any one encounter can be anything from five minutes to a couple of hours. As in mainstream wrestling, the winner is the person who can pin his opponent to the ground for a specified number of seconds.

OTHER TURKISH SPORTS

HUNTING AND SHOOTING This was once more than just a sport, as the hunted game was a valuable source of food for peasants. A notable exception to this is boar hunting, because the boar, being a pig, cannot be eaten by Moslems.

CIRIT ("gerh-IT") This is a traditional Turkish sport that is becoming increasingly difficult to observe. It is played during the winter on horseback, with the rider carrying a wooden javelin. The object of the game is to throw the javelin and hit one's opponent. Each hit earns a point, and the winner is the rider who first achieves a set number of points.

SKIING Turkey is not usually associated with skiing, although there are a number of ski resorts in the country. The sport is becoming increasingly popular with Turks. The oldest established resort is Mount Olympus in northwest Anatolia.

Cirit, the "javelin game" of daredevil horsemanship, is a sport where wooden javelins are thrown at horsemen of the opposing team to gain a point. The game is played mainly in eastern Turkey.

FESTIVALS

TWO OF TURKEY'S most important festivals are religious in nature. One marks the end of Ramazan, the most significant event in the Moslem calendar, while the other marks the end of the pilgrimage to Mecca. Both are major public holidays with shops and offices closed for up to four days.

Alongside the religious events, there are a number of interesting cultural festivals, such as the one dedicated to greased wrestling that takes place near Edirne every year in the early summer.

SEKER BAYRAM

Seker Bayram marks the end of Ramazan, the Moslem period of fasting that lasts one month. During the month of Ramazan, no food or drink is allowed to pass one's lips between the hours of sunrise and sunset. Not surprisingly, the end of the fasting period is characterized by family feasts. The general atmosphere is one of celebration, and it is close to the spirit of Easter in its combination of a religious event with purely secular festivities.

Seker Bayram is a time of family reunions. Children are always delighted by the festival because presents and candy are handed out.

Opposite and above: **Festivals in Turkey are invariably accompanied by music and dancing. Each region in Turkey has its own special folk dance and costume.**

KURBAN BAYRAM

Kurban Bayram is also known as the Feast of the Sacrifice. Many Turkish families commemorate the day by slaughtering a sheep. The killing of the animal is a sacrifice recalling the sheep that Ibrahim sacrificed in place of his son Ishmael, as the Koranic version of the story found in the Bible tells. The Judeo-Christian version also tells of how Abraham was willing to sacrifice his son, Isaac, in obedience to God's command, and how God substituted a sheep at the last moment.

Buying a whole sheep to sacrifice is often too expensive for small families in cities, and there is too much meat left over. Butchers will sell part of a sheep instead.

CALENDAR OF FESTIVALS AND SPECIAL DAYS

New Year's Day **(January 1)** This is a public holiday marked by processions and sports events.

Seker Bayram and Kurban Bayram These two important events are fixed by the Moslem lunar calendar. This means that the exact dates vary from one year to the next. In 1993, Seker Bayram takes place on March 24 to 26, while Kurban Bayram occurs on June 1 to 4.

National Independence and Children's Day **(April 23)** is the anniversary of the opening of the first Grand National Assembly in Ankara.

Spring Day **(May 1)** This is the equivalent of Labor Day in the United States, and May Day in Britain. It is not, however, a public holiday. Trade unions hold their own celebrations.

Youth Day **(May 19)** is the anniversary of Mustafa Kemal's landing at Samsun at the beginning of his campaign in Anatolia.

Victory Day **(August 30)** marks the final rout of invading Greek forces in 1922.

Republic Day **(October 28 and 29)** Events on these days commemorate the proclamation of the Turkish republic by Ataturk.

Anniversary of the death of Ataturk November 10 is a day of mourning, and places of entertainment are closed and no alcohol is sold. It is not an official public holiday. General business carries on normally until 9:05 a.m., when the whole country stops to observe a minute's silence, as this was the time of Ataturk's death.

CULTURAL FESTIVALS

Every year in the middle of summer, the prestigious International Istanbul Festival takes place. Visitors come from all over the world to see this monthlong festival of the arts. Major events include performances of European and Turkish operas, ballet, and music. Part of the appeal of these performances is the fact that they are staged in places such as the Topkapi Palace.

Each year, in Konya, there is a festival that, although deeply religious in origin, has a cultural appeal to observers of all creeds. The Mevlana Festival is one of the few occasions when the dance of the Whirling Dervishes can be seen. In recent years, performances of this enchanting dance can also be witnessed in Istanbul around the same time, December 14 to 17.

Above: **A festival is staged in a historical site in Turkey. The backdrop lends a sense of drama to the performance.**

Opposite: **The Spoon Dance consists of gaily dressed male and female dancers clicking out the dance rhythm with a pair of wooden spoons in each hand.**

The annual Kirkpinar Festival takes place near Edirne, a town very close to the Greek border. It usually starts at the beginning of July. One of the oldest cultural festivals in Turkey, it is a series of tournaments leading to the declaration of the champion greased wrestler. A popular story places the origin of the event back in the time of Suleiman. Returning with 40 men from a battle in 1360, Suleiman chose to camp near Edirne. To pass the time, the men began wrestling in pairs. The two men who emerged as finalists were so equally matched that they wrestled until both collapsed in utter exhaustion and died. Buried by their comrades, they were soon forgotten until the following year, when the graves were visited by some of Suleiman's men. On the site, they found 40 *kirkpinar*, or springs of fresh water. Now, over 600 hundred years later, men still wrestle on that spot for the prestigious title of overall champion. As many as a thousand men enter the festival, and the final winner is sure to win fame and fortune.

Folk festivals are regularly held in Turkey. These provide the best opportunities to see the folk dances and hear the folk music that was once an integral part of village life. Nowadays, sadly, such events are becoming

REGIONAL FOLK DANCES

THE SPOON DANCE This dance takes place in the area around the town of Silifke on the Mediterranean coast. Male and female dancers are dressed in the colors of the rainbow, and the dance rhythm is clicked out with a pair of wooden spoons in each hand.

THE SWORD AND SHIELD DANCE OF BURSA This dance represents the conquest of the city of Bursa by Ottoman forces. The dancers are all men, dressed in the battle gear of the early Ottoman warriors. There is no musical accompaniment as such, and martial sound effects are produced by the clashing of swords and shields as dancers hurl themselves in the air.

THE HORON DANCE This distinctive dance is performed in the Black Sea coast area. Dancers, all male, are dressed in black with trimmings of silver. They link arms and shake in a quivering motion to the vibrations of a local musical instrument that bears a resemblance to the violin.

increasingly rare. Both the dances and the accompanying music originated on the steppes of Asia before the Turkish tribes were converted to Islam. The dances are characterized by lively exuberant movements, and each region in Turkey has its own special dance and costumes.

FOOD

TURKEY IS FAMOUS for its food. It can justly claim to be one of the world's great cuisines, partly because of the variety of food available. The different climates in the country, and the fact that it is surrounded by the sea on three sides, means that fresh meat, fish, and vegetables are available throughout the year. Turkey is particularly famous for its smaller dishes that are served before and after the main dish. Appetizers come in an astonishing variety of forms, and equally mouth-watering are Turkish desserts served after a meal.

TURKISH DELIGHTS

Meze ("MAY-zay") are Turkish hors d'oeuvres (extra dishes served as a relish before the main meal). They are made from meat and fish and are often enjoyed by Turks over a glass of wine or raki. Some of the most delicious ones are made from eggplant, zucchini, or pickled vegetables. Each meze will have its own name. *Sigara boregi*, for instance, is a tightly rolled cheese pastry. *Imam bayildi* is made from cooked eggplant filled with onions and tomatoes and served cold. Imam bayildi translates as "the imam swooned," the suggestion being that the dish was so delicious that the imam (the prayer leader of the mosque) almost fainted at the sight and taste of it.

Vegetables are not mere accompaniments to meat but are prepared and served as delicacies in themselves. Many vegetables, such as tomatoes, peppers, eggplants, pumpkins, and squash, are stuffed with rice and meat. When Turks order their vegetables in a restaurant, they will ask for *dolmasi* if they want them stuffed in this way.

Opposite and above: **Turkey produces a wide range of fruits and vegetables. They are used imaginatively in a variety of dishes.**

Surrounded on three
sides by the sea, Turkey
has abundant fish. For
those living by the sea,
fishing is their chief
means of livelihood.

With a ready supply of fresh fish, it is not surprising to find fish dishes being served in a variety of ways. Swordfish is often grilled on a skewer and mixed with pieces of pepper and onion. This swordfish kebab is called *kilicsis* ("kihl-ITCH-shish"). Any town near the coast will have a plentiful supply of fresh sardines and tuna. They are eaten as snacks or as a light lunch with thinly baked bread. Bluefish are caught in the Bosporus from small boats carrying lamps to attract the fish.

There are significant regional variations in Turkish cuisine. Farming families in Anatolia have what is probably the least varied diet, being heavily dependent on buckwheat, soup, and stewed meat. The coastal area around the Black Sea, on the other hand, has the benefit of fresh anchovies and locally grown nuts. Walnuts are crushed and turned into a puree and seasoned with pepper before being dripped over chicken. Known as Circassian chicken, this is another Turkish concoction that has become internationally known and appreciated.

In the southeast, the proximity to Arab lands has influenced the choice and style of food. Chickpeas and other legumes, such as peas, beans, and lentils, are staples, and the kebabs are hotter and spicier.

ETIQUETTE AND TABOOS

Etiquette allows, and sometimes expects, a customer in a restaurant to go into the kitchen and inspect the food being prepared and cooked. There will usually be at least one large saucepan containing the main meat dish of the day, and it is perfectly acceptable to taste the food. The vegetables and rice will be open to inspection in other saucepans nearby. Individual requests are welcomed if, for example, someone wants vegetables cooked in a certain way.

A family sits down to a meal. For Moslems, eating pork is strictly forbidden.

The only taboo that is widespread concerns the eating of pork. Islam strictly forbids the eating of this meat, and even cooking utensils should not be used if they previously came into contact with the forbidden meat. Islam also prohibits the drinking of alcohol, but beer and wine are generally available and consumed by many Turks. There is certainly no taboo about requesting an alcoholic drink . Even in more conservative Moslem areas, a restaurant will serve alcohol to non-Moslem customers.

In conservative areas, unaccompanied women are sometimes ushered into the family parlor area, either upstairs or behind a curtain on the same floor as the restaurant. Unaccompanied women are not expected to visit a *meyhane*, the Turkish tavern or pub. These are strictly male preserves, where serious drinking is the order of the day.

TYPICAL MEALS

Breakfast A Turkish breakfast is a modest affair compared to the traditional American breakfast. It usually consists of bread, cheese, and a few olives. Small cafés also serve *borek*, a pastry filled with bits of mincemeat or cheese, or a soup seasoned with lemon.

Lunch A favorite lunch is leaves of cabbage stuffed with pieces of chopped meat and rice, and served with yogurt. A form of pizza, known as *pide*, is also eaten for lunch with various toppings of sausage, cheese, or egg.

Evening Meal This is the main meal of the day for most Turks. It often begins with a soup of rice and vegetables or lentils. The main dish will be *shish kebab* or perhaps chicken with rice.

Although shish kebab is the most widely known Turkish dish, it does in fact come in a number of variations. *Adana kebab* is more spicy, sprinkled over the top with purple sumac herb. Kebab dishes are usually eaten with a slice of thin bread.

In the countryside, the evening meal is often based on boiled buckwheat served with fresh vegetables. This common dish is known as *bulgur pilavi* ("bool-GOOR PIHL-ah-vih"). As an accompaniment, yogurt is commonly mixed with water and salt, and poured into a glass as a drink.

Above: **A *pide* dish.**

KEBABS

Shish kebab is a Turkish dish that is known all over the world. It is made out of cubes of lamb roasted on skewers over a charcoal fire. The origins of this dish go back to the pre-Islamic era in Turkey's past when the Turks lived as nomads in the plains of Central Asia. Living a pastoral existence as shepherds meant that lamb was always available, and lamb remains the staple meat in the country's cuisine. Besides being grilled as kebabs, lamb is also stewed or minced and made into meatballs. Mutton is roasted or cooked in a casserole.

Another well-known kebab is *doner kebab*. Lamb meat is seasoned with various spices, then compressed into a large inverted cone that is turned on a vertical rotating grill in front of hot coals. When a customer requests a doner kebab, thin slices of the mutton are finely carved off the meat on the rotating grill and served with melted butter on pita bread.

Above: **Snack stalls offering all kinds of delicious food are found all over the streets of Turkey. They are patronized by Turks from all walks of life.**

Left: ***Doner kebab***, **lamb grilled on a vertical spit, is one of Turkey's favorite foods. It is found in nearly all Turkish restaurants around the world.**

EGGPLANT AND YOGURT

Eggplants, *patlican* in Turkish, are called the "king of vegetables" by Turks. There are said to be over a hundred recipes based on this vegetable. Some of them have interesting names, such as *sultan beyendi,* which means "what is pleasing to the sultan."

Yogurt is a word that Turkey has contributed to the English language, and it is an ingredient in many meals and refreshments. One very tasty snack, called *manti,* is a meat-filled ravioli that is soaked in yogurt and spicy oil.

YOGURT WITH GARLIC

Ingredients
8 fluid ounces of plain yogurt
A pinch of salt
1 clove of garlic, mashed
A pinch of ground black pepper
2 teaspoons of olive oil

Whisk the yogurt in a bowl until smooth and creamy. Add all the remaining ingredients and beat in to mix thoroughly. Cover and keep cool while preparing the eggplant.

FRIED EGGPLANT WITH YOGURT SAUCE

Ingredients
1 eggplant
1 teaspoon of salt
1 tablespoon of lemon juice
Olive oil
Yogurt

Cut the eggplant into slices and lay them flat on the table before sprinkling with salt and lemon. Turn the slices over and repeat on the other side. Leave the eggplant slices for about 20 minutes, then drain and leave to dry.

Heat the olive oil in a pan and, when hot, add the eggplant slices. Fry gently on each side for a couple of minutes and, when the slices begin to turn reddish-brown, serve them on a plate with the yogurt as a sauce.

DESSERTS AND SWEETS

The true Turkish delights are the desserts and sweets. Baklava is a typical treat that consists of a small roll of fried pastry made rich with crushed nuts soaked in honey. There are many variations of this sweet mixture of sugar, flour, nuts, and butter. The window display of any *pastane* (pastry shop) usually contains a tempting selection.

Other desserts are more elaborate. They include a mixture of semolina starch, milk, and a highly refined mixture made from a chicken breast that has been boiled and strained. The whole pudding is then covered with cinnamon. Other desserts that Turks love to prepare and eat are *lokma* (round doughnuts in syrup), *krem karamel* (caramel custard), and *kabak tatlisi* (slices of pumpkin in syrup).

TURKISH DELIGHTS

Ingredients
Half a cup of rosewater
2 cups of sugar
2 tablespoons of gelatin

One quarter cup of cold water
Half a cup of orange juice
One quarter cup of lemon juice
Confectioners' sugar

Mix the water with the sugar, and heat to 255°F. Remove from the heat. Soften the gelatin in a quarter cup of cold water for 5 minutes before adding the gelatin mixture to the cooked syrup. Add the other juices and stir and strain through a sieve. Pour into a buttered square pan and let stand until the mixture is firm. Turn out and cut into squares, and roll in the confectioners' sugar.

Turkish tea. About 1 million tons of tea are picked annually in Turkey. A common sight is women carrying large loads of tea leaves in baskets strapped to their backs. Immediately after the leaves are picked, they are taken to tea factories for fermenting and drying.

DRINKS

Tea, called *cay* ("CHA-hy"), is grown along the Black Sea coast and is the national drink of Turkey. It is prepared in an elaborate double boiler type container called a samovar, and poured into tiny glasses before being diluted to suit one's taste. It is always drunk without milk.

Although Islamic fundamentalists campaign against the easy availability of alcohol, beer and wine are drunk throughout Turkey. There are vineyards across western Anatolia, and Turkish wine can be of very good quality. There are over a hundred varieties of red and white wine.

The most commonly drunk alcoholic beverage, however, is raki. It is the national aperitif (alcoholic appetizer) and is usually served with ice and diluted with water. Raki clouds over when water is added to it, giving it the popular name of "lion's milk."

Moslems often drink *sira*, a very tasty nonalcoholic grape drink. It is commonly available in restaurants that do not serve alcohol. There are many other traditional beverages. One that contains medicinal properties is *salep*. It is made from hot milk and the roots of a wild orchid found in the coastal areas of the country. Sprinkled with cinnamon, salep is a favorite remedy for a cold or the flu.

TURKISH COFFEE

Coffee was introduced to Europe by the Turks, the story being that the Austrian defenders of Vienna found barrels of the stuff after the Ottoman invaders gave up trying to capture the city. Turkish coffee, known as *kahve* ("KAH-veh"), is made from very finely ground coffee beans with just a touch of cardamom added. The taste is thick and strong, so it is generously sweetened with sugar. The heavy coffee grounds sink to the bottom of each cup and are not meant to be consumed.

To make authentic Turkish coffee, a *tanaka* is necessary. This is a narrow-necked and long-handled pot that helps create the characteristic froth. A tanaka can be purchased from Middle Eastern stores in North America. The coffee itself is served from demitasse cups that are about one-third the size of a regular coffee cup. Turks have a different name for Western coffee, *kahve ala frengi.*

RECIPE FOR TURKISH COFFEE

Ingredients
2 to 4 teaspoons of sugar, to taste
2 whole cardamom pods
4 heaped teaspoons of Turkish coffee

Place four demitasse cups of water into the tanaka, and bring to a boil with the sugar and cardamom added. When the mixture is boiling, stir in the coffee. Remove the tanaka from the heat as soon as the froth begins rising to the top. When the froth has subsided, put the tanaka back on the heat and then remove once more when the froth returns to the surface. Repeat this process a third time. Spoon the froth into the cups, and pour the coffee over the froth. Remove the cardamom pods. When the froth rises to the top of the cups, it is ready for drinking.

BULGARIA

GREECE

Edirne

Bosporus

Istanbul

Uskudar

Izmit Valley

Dardanelles

Gallipoli

Marmara

Canakkale

Iznik

Bursa

Troy (Ruins)

Sakarya

Zonguldak

Eregli

PONTIC

BLACK SEA

Sinop

Samsun

Kizil Irmak

Bogazkoy

Hattusas (Ruins)

Ankara

CENTRAL

PLATEAU

Pergamum (Ruins)

Manisa

Izmir

Gediz

Ephesus (Ruins)

Menderes

Aydin

Pamukkale

Miletus (Ruins)

Didyma (Ruins)

AEGEAN SEA

Lake Tuz

Kayseri

Cappadocia (Ruins)

Konya

Mamaris

Rhodes

Fethiye

Antalya

Alanya

Karaman

Seyhan

TAURUS MOUNTAINS

Adana

Mersin

TURKEY

MEDITERRANEAN SEA

CYPRUS

A B C D

1

2

3

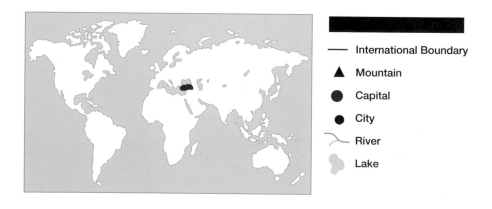

— International Boundary

▲ Mountain

● Capital

● City

〜 River

Lake

E   F   G

GEORGIA

N

• Hopa
• Ardesen
Trabzon Rize • Pazar

ARMENIA

Yesil Irmak
MOUNTAINS

Kars •

Erzincan
• Erzurum

Divrigi

Mt. Ararat ▲

Dogubeyazit •

• Elazig

Lake
Van

Malatya

• Van

IRAN

• Diyarbakir

Euphrates   Tigris .

Elazig
• Urfa   • Mardin

SYRIA   IRAQ

Karaman C3
Kars F1
Kayseri D2
Kizil Irmak River D1
Konya C2

Lake Tuz C2
Lake Van F2

Malatya E2
Mardin F3
Manisa A2
Marmara A1
Marmaris A3
Menderes B2
Mersin D3
Miletus (Ruins) A2
Mt. Ararat G2

Pamukkale D2
Pazar F1
Pergamum (Ruins) A2
Pontic Mountains D1

Rhodes A3
Rize F1

Seyhan River D3
Sakarya River B1
Samsun D1
Sinop D1

Taurus Mountains C3
Tigris River F3
Trabzon E1
Troy (Ruins) A1

Urfa E3
Uskudar B1

Van G2

Yesil Irmak River E1

Zonguldak C1

Adana D3
Alanya C3
Ankara C2
Antalya B3
Ardesen F1
Aydin A2

Bogazkoy D2
Bosporus B1
Bursa B1

Canakkale A1
Cappadocia (Ruins) D2

Dardanelles A1
Didyma (Ruins) A2
Divrigi E2
Diyarbakir F2
Dogubeyazit G2

Edirne A1
Elazig E2
Ephesus (Ruins) A2
Eregli C1
Erzincan E2
Erzurum F2
Euphrates River E3

Fethiye B3

Gallipoli A1
Gediz River B2

Hattusas (Ruins) D2
Hopa F1

Istanbul B1
Izmir A2
Izmit Valley B1
Iznik B1

QUICK NOTES

LAND AREA
309,000 square miles

POPULATION
57 million

CAPITAL
Ankara

MAJOR CITIES
Istanbul, Izmir, Adana

GEOGRAPHIC REGIONS
Mediterranean coast, West Anatolia, East Anatolia, Southwest Anatolia, Central Anatolia, Black Sea coast, Marmara and Aegean coasts, Thrace

HIGHEST POINT
Mt. Ararat (16,786 feet)

MAJOR LAKE
Lake Van

MAJOR RIVERS
Tigris, Euphrates, Kizil Irmak, Yesil Irmak, Sakarya

LANGUAGE
Turkish

RELIGION
Moslem (99%)

CURRENCY
Turkish Lira
($1 = 600 Turkish lira)

MAIN EXPORTS
Textiles, agricultural products, iron and nonferrous metals, food, leather, and hides

MAIN IMPORTS
Crude oil, machinery, chemicals, iron and steel, electrical appliances

LEADERS IN POLITICS
Turgut Ozal—President of Turkey (1989-)
Mustafa Kemal Ataturk—Founder and first president of Turkish republic (1923-1938)
Suleiman the Magnificent—Ottoman sultan whose reign (1520-1566) witnessed the highest achievements and geographical expansion of the Ottoman empire.

GLOSSARY

gece kondu ("GEDJ-erh KOHN-doo") Squatters' dwellings around the big cities.

dolmus ("dohl-MERHS") A communal taxi/bus that follows a set route but stops wherever required.

hamam ("hahm-AHM") Turkish steam bath.

harem The women's quarters in Ottoman residences.

imam Often the prayer leader at a mosque, although an imam can also be a person of considerable spiritual authority.

Ramazan The Moslem month of fasting and prayer; known as Ramadan outside of Turkey.

Sufi A follower of one of the mystical branches of Islam.

yayla ("YAHR-lah") Rural settlements built of stone to half their height and then completed in timber.

BIBLIOGRAPHY

Davison, Roderic H.: *Turkey: A Short History,* Eothen, UK, 1988.

Feinstein, Stephen C.: *Turkey in Pictures,* Lerner Publications Company, Minneapolis, MN, 1988.

Freely, John: *The Western Shores of Turkey,* J. Murray, London, 1988.

Spencer, William: *The Land and People of Turkey,* Lippincott, New York, NY, 1989.

Turkish Tourist Information Office: 821 UN Plaza, 4th Floor, New York, NY 10017.

INDEX